AF579975

TOMORROW'S HEADLINES TODAY

Other books by Sybil Leek:

DIARY OF A WITCH

SYBIL LEEK'S ASTROLOGICAL GUIDE TO SUCCESSFUL EVERYDAY LIVING

MY LIFE IN ASTROLOGY

TOMORROW'S

SYBIL LEEK

HEADLINES TODAY

Prentice-Hall, Inc., Englewood Cliffs, N.J.

Printed in the United States of America
Prentice-Hall International, Inc., London
Prentice-Hall of Australia, Pty. Ltd., Sydney
Prentice-Hall of Canada, Ltd., Toronto
Prentice-Hall of India Private Ltd., New Delhi
Prentice-Hall of Japan, Inc., Tokyo

---

10 9 8 7 6 5 4 3 2 1

Library of Congress Cataloging in Publication Data
Leek, Sybil.
Tomorrow's headlines today.
1. Astrology. I. Title.
BF1708.1.L42 133.5 74–7108
ISBN 0–13–924787–4

To
MARTIN CAIDIN
The Typical Aquarian Age Man

CONTENTS

TOMORROW'S HEADLINES TODAY

1

GRASS ROOTS TO THE ASTROLOGICAL GRAPEVINE

Astrology was once the ancient religion based on the stars, consistently followed in every country of the world, yet in the last few years a subtle war has been declared against it by both church and science.

Scientists do not want to realize that our truly ancient ancestors were not creatures merely one step above animal life, conscious only of superstitions. Yet the further back in history we go, the higher the degree of civilization we unearth and the greater the refinement of art and learning. The Chaldeans, Aryans, and Assyrians; the Cushites of southern Arabia; the Phoenicians, Phrygarians, the Pelasgians, and the Chinese all were skilled in the arts and sciences, and all built cities, some of which had a highly developed system of government. The early Egyptians and Babylonians had a written language and were well versed in astronomy, astrology, medicine, and the use of iron. The

Chaldeans, Persians, Hindus, Chinese, and Egyptians all had a seven-day week, the days—even as today—being named after the seven known planets; all nations held Sunday sacred to the same planet. At the same time, Mexico and South and Central America all had a well-developed astronomical-astrological religion.

In the light of history, it seems inconceivable that today's so-called learned men should judge astrology on the preconceived idea that our ancestors were ignorant and superstitious. Even more preposterous is the idea that the planets cannot have any influence on the character and actions of men. Back when the church and science were having their private war, scientists were quick to advise churchmen that the truth of a statement should be demonstrated experimentally, that it should not be determined by speculation alone. The modern astrologer agrees, and today thousands of keen students of astrology are experimentally investigating the subject. The majority of them are finding proof that the positions and movements of the planets *do* correspond to characteristics and events in the life of man—even as previously recorded by our ancient ancestors.

Scientists of the future will wonder why we of the space age were so stupid as to let personal prejudices cause us to neglect the investigation of astrology, which is as thoroughly experimental and as scientifically exact as chemistry, botany, or physics. Our "uneducated" ancestors in China recorded a series of eclipses in 2169 B.C. The Chinese were acquainted with both solar and lunar calendars, as well as the arts of civilized life. Herodotus says that the Egyptians had recorded planetary and solar observations for 11,340 years, had seen four great solar cycles of 25,920 years each, and had records of a time when the ecliptic was perpendicular to the Equator. (The ecliptic is the orbit described by the the earth around the sun in a year's time.) At the ecliptic's present rate of decrease, that should have taken place about 480,000 years ago—about the time of the Trinil Man, who scientists tell us was the man with the least brain capacity. If scientists are right in this, astrology can point to the drastic climatic conditions that caused this race to degenerate to little more than a beast.

In 1700 B.C., so archaeologists say, the Babylonians recorded in King Sargon's library their observations of the god Bel. This work is in 70 parts, each composed of a number of small earthen tablets, with the records, in cuneiform characters, punched into them. Yet we have evidence that both astronomy and a written language were brought to Babylonia by the Akkadians, who were already conversant with the civilized arts and sciences, including medicine evidently considered to be equally as important. The earliest inhabitants of Peru and Mexico understood astronomy, and surviving temples show evidence of an astronomical religion. They were also conversant with cycles which only an immense period of recorded observations would enable them to demonstrate experimentally. It is no coincidence that the Pleiades are known by the natives of every land in the world, even in the islands of the Pacific, as signifying a group of seven sisters; or that the constellation of the great bear was known to the Iroquois Indians as Okouairi (the Indian name for bear) and to the Greeks as Arctos Megale, the Great Bear. These and a thousand other parallels suggest that the astronomy and astrology known to all ancient nations must have been derived from a pre-existing and higher civilization.

When various nations at times were isolated and unable to communicate with each other, each retained the most significant facts in their own traditions and then interwove them with local history and with traits and characteristics indigenous to each nation. Richard Hinckley Allen, an acknowledged scholar and authority on origins, wrote:

> Probably every nation on earth has had a solar zodiac in some form, generally one [composed] of animals. Even in Rhodesia, the aboriginal Mashona Land of South Africa, there has recently been found a stone tablet 38 inches in diameter, with the circle of the zodiacal signs on the edge; and the early Mandean tradition makes its figures children of their creative spirits Ur Nad Ruha.

The same author reports the use of the lunar zodiac also in ancient Arabia, China, India, Khiva, Bokhara, Egypt, and Persia.

Maybe it is time to ask why we now have so little of the wisdom possessed by our ancestors of even a few thousand years ago. The answer may well lie in a history of bigoted fanaticism on the part of both religion and science.

When the Brahmins gained power in India, they destroyed a great deal of the literature of Hindustan that did not support their own doctrines. In 332 B.C., Alexander the Great founded the Alexandrian Library and spent enormous sums of money collecting literary works from all over the world. What he could not purchase outright, his agents were instructed to copy and send to Alexandria. In the time of Julius Caesar there were 700,000 works in the library. In A.D. 296, Diocletian—motivated by religious fanaticism—burned all the esoteric works of the Egyptians, including priceless volumes on astrology, magic, and alchemy.

There were some 300,000 literary works at Constantinople, which were destroyed by Emperor Leo III of Isauria in the interests of Christianity. What the Christians left of the Alexandrian Library was finished off by Muhammed ("If these books agree with the Koran, they are unnecessary; if not, they are pernicious"), thus completing the destruction of every record and piece of learning. The Romans had destroyed the records of Carthage and Spain, and in turn the Gauls destroyed the Annals of Rome. Even works of art were not exempt, and we find Byzantine edicts issued by Leo the Isaurian for the destruction of all statuary and every image of the past because they might interfere with the spread of Catholicism.

The Arabians carried some of the wisdom of Egypt and secreted it in the desert; some ultimately found its way to Europe. About A.D.1500, Cardinal Zimenes burned all the Arabian manuscripts found in Spain, which was then the cultural center of Europe. The Moslems overran the East, destroying every book and record from Benares to Bactria and Syria. Soon after America was discovered, the Spanish grand inquisitor Torquemada at Salamanca, and the Spanish priests in Central America, Mexico, and Peru, put a determined effort into the destruction of recorded wisdom.

The present war on astrology is not new, for there has been an uninterrupted war on the occult sciences for over 2,000 years, every generation vying with the preceding one in an effort to eliminate ancient wisdom. So with the exception of a few secret schools of thought and philosophy, the only shards of the ideas held by our ancestors found today are those recorded by structures of such colossal size that it was impossible to destroy them. It is to these that we should now turn in an effort to understand more about astrology.

The source of all warmth, energy, and power known on earth is the Sun, a universal symbol of creative energy. The ancients had recognized it as the center of the solar system. All life and light, and the intangible reflection of these as love, come from the Sun, the solar father and the most comprehensive symbol of the omniscient, omnipotent, and omnipresent. The Sun is a much older symbol of a deity than a man on the cross.

The ancients also recognized a still greater center about which our universe is moving, and they located its relative position as a great spiritual Sun, not visible to the mortal eye: They discovered a fountain of creative energy in man himself. Initiative, intellectual forces, vitality, and love are fed by man's creative virility. There can be no life, intelligence, nor action in the universe that is not an offspring of polarity, the affinity of a positive for a negative, and it is on the laws of polarity that astrology is based.

Polarity is also linked with sex, the one universal law of manifestation inasmuch as attraction produces a third element. Obelisks and upright towers were erected as symbols of creative power and as emblems of the Sun—source of universal creative power—and they were both solar and phallic in conception.

The huge stone structures called megaliths, which were erected by prehistoric races, are still found in all parts of the world. There are 2,582 in France, 2,000 in the Orkney Isles, 2,199 in a single district in India, and the total is almost beyond calculation.

Menhirs were huge single stones placed upright, the obelisk being the finest finished example. There are numerous obelisks in Egypt, Assyria, Peru, Mexico, and Brittany—each erected as a symbol to the Sun, the upright position symbolizing the direction from which the Sun's fiercest rays fall on the earth. They are phallic insofar as the Sun is a universal phallic emblem.

Even the maypole dance is a remnant of Sun worship, derived directly from the sacred dances around the menhirs. "Ma" is the root of the word "matter" in all languages, and from it is derived "matrix" and "mother." The month of Ma(y) is the one in which the Sun, having crossed the vernal equinox and gained virile energy in the sign of the Ram, enters the first earth or matrix sign, Taurus. Astrologically, Taurus is regarded as the exaltation of the Moon or mother, whereas Aries is the exaltation of the Sun or father. Taurus is the sign in which the solar father warms the earth, the mother, so that she may become fruitful. The ancients knew this to be a good time for plowing and planting, and Taurus has always been associated with the fruits of the earth.

The sacred dances around the maypole were in celebration of the Sun-father and the earth-mother, and the participants danced in a pantomime of the planets. The maypole ceremony is still practiced in Europe and America, but many people are unaware that it was known in India, Egypt, and Persia. It is also performed by the aborigines of the Yucatán, where it was handed down from the Maya, and it is still danced at the time of the vernal equinox.

This traditional May dance is essentially the same in all countries. In Ireland it is customary for the men to wear white shirts during the dance, and the Maya also wear white. White is a symbol of the pure union of the Sun with the earth, and wearing this color was a means of conveying the idea that parenthood should be entered into purely as a solemn and sacred rite. The spring festival which the ancients dedicated to the Sun's renewed vigor in fructifying the earth—in preparation for bringing forth the harvest which would sustain man in the coming dark days of winter—was also the occasion to show gratitude by the giving of gifts. Since the solar father crossing the equator from the south brought the gift of renewed life through verdure, blossoms, and ultimately human fertility, it was thought fitting to reciprocate. Originally the vernal gift was also associated with sacrifice, but now this practice has been modified throughout the world, its most notable relic being the giving of Easter gifts or May baskets.

An elaboration of the simple menhir is the round tower, also found throughout the world. They are all similar in construction, built of stone, usually with a single entrance some distance from the ground. There are 150 of these round towers in Ireland alone, ranging from 70 to 130 feet in height and from 8 to 15 feet in diameter, each with a single opening some 20 feet from the ground. Ireland was the nearest European land to Atlantis, and in ancient Sanskrit writing Ireland is called Hyrania, meaning Island of Sun Worship. The chief god of Ireland in Sanskrit times was Baal, or Bel, god of the Sun, from whom Belfast was named.

Americans can find round towers in Rhode Island, one in the Mancos Valley in southwestern Colorado, and another in the Yucatán. There are also round towers in the Shetland Islands, the Isle of Man, Scotland, and Corsica. The leaning tower of Pisa in Italy is a campanile, or belltower, patterned after the round towers of Sicily, Algeria, Sardinia, Arabia, and India.

These round towers were monuments to the Sun, but they also served a practical purpose as observatories, in which instruments for astronomical observations were kept. The druids, who were the oldest inhabitants of Ireland in historical times, were astrologers of no mean ability. Caesar tells us that the druids taught many things about the form and dimension of the earth, the size and arrangement of the different parts of the heavens, and the various motions of the planets. Plutarch records that the druids claimed the Moon was furrowed; and according to Hecataeus, the druids taught that the Moon was a great body like the earth and that there were mountains on it. This opinion was far in advance of that of the Greeks and Romans, who were content to believe that the Moon was a flat, shining disc.

Other universal stone monuments were the conical dome-shaped towers called talayots. These are found in Italy and Sardinia, and in the Balearic Islands there are seven called the navetas. They are shaped like an upturned boat—the general construction is dome-like—but with a single entrance so small and close to the ground that the only way to enter is by crawling on the belly! The walls are often as much as 18 feet thick, completely shutting off light from the outside. The ventilation is negligible, and they could never have been used as dwellings. In front of many of the talayots are circles of surrounding stones, sometimes sculpted in the shape of a woman's breast. These are the cromlechs; we know that they were dedicated to the Moon and that they are monuments to femininity, the receptive principle of nature. That so many ancient people thought it fitting to erect huge stones to the glorification of the Sun-father and Moon-mother principles is no coincidence, since these concepts are constant throughout the world.

Another ancient stone monument linked with astrological lore are the dolmens. These monuments consist of two or more upright stones supporting a single large, flat slab of stone. The dolmens can be found from the Atlantic Ocean to the Ural Mountains, from Russia to the Pacific Ocean, from Siberia to India, as well as in Peru, Japan, Patagonia, and England. There is a famous one near Dorchester, England, consisting of nine upright stones supporting a stone table more than 27 feet in circumference and nearly 3 feet thick. How a people not possessing cantilever cranes could raise these stone slabs and place them on upright pillars is a marvel which has not yet been fully accounted for scientifically. The dolmens are identical in shape to the fifth Hebrew letter "he," and leading one to believe that there was an esoteric thought behind their structure. In fact, each stone monument can be best understood in terms of esoteric thought—and behind the esoteric thought of the ancient people was always the religion of the stars, a link with astrology.

The flat slab, table-like, is a plane and is always supported *above* the earth, signifying, of course, a plane above the earth. The supports form a doorway, which is a place through which one passes from one place to another. So the dolmens present a tangible idea that our so-called primitive ancestors knew something about a plane of life above the earth which man can enter in due course. But the dolmen is an offspring of the round tower and the dome. The round tower is the spiritual principle; the dome is the earthly matrix in which the immaculate conception takes place—these concepts were celebrated with due solemnity in the maypole dance when the Sun was in Taurus.

The cromlechs, found in Europe, Asia, America, and Africa, also have a special significance. These circular or eliptical rows of stone or mounds of earth symbolize and sometimes record the orbital motion of the stellar bodies; religiously, they signify that those who erected them were aware that the spirit of man, like the circle, is without beginning and end, and that man comes from the infinite and returns to it again. The significance of the circular zodiac is irrevocably linked with man's desire to erect indestructible stone monuments to his religious beliefs, which in the early days were also linked to his interest in celestial bodies.

Astrologers today take pride in saying that the science has been in existence for over 6,000 years. In this I believe them to be wrong, for there is enough evidence on the earth to indicate that astrology was known long before there was any attempt to record history. There is also evidence that there was a high degree of civilization before man was thought to have existed on earth. The fact that ancient man recorded and presumably understood solar-lunar cycles well enough to compute projections of them far into the future is provocative to say the least.

It is rapidly becoming more than a theory that all the civilizations of the world had a common source in Atlantis. The implications of author Ignatius Donnelly in his scholarly work on Atlantis are constantly being substantiated by the discovery of written records as well as in the indestructible records on stone. For instance, in stone carvings made by the Maya, as well as their Troane Manuscript and the Dresden, Madrid and Paris codices, there are records of the destruction by earthquake and the submergence of a huge island in the Atlantic Ocean. The Troane Manuscript states that Mu (Atlantis) disappeared 8,160 years before the manuscript was written, and this corroborates the records of the Egyptians concerning the same event. Early in the twentieth century Dr. A. Le Plongeon translated inscriptions written in the Maya language and compared them with those of Egyptian origin and Maya characters on the walls of the Pyramid of Xochimilco in Mexico. He found the statement that the pyramid was erected for the purpose of perpetuating the knowledge of the destruction of Mu. He also concluded from the written text that the pyramid was an exact model of the sacred hill of Atlantis, described in detail by Plato, who gained his knowledge of it from the Egyptians. Dr. Le Plongeon also states that one-third of the Maya language is similar to Greek, and some of it is clearly like Assyrian.

It seems very likely that present civilizations and all religious thoughts in the world today were derived from the civilization and religion of Atlantis, the fabulous island which sank in a great cataclysm beneath the surface of the Atlantic Ocean. There is much evidence that once there was an island of Atlantis, that there was a deluge, that spirit communion is possible, and that the mind can commune with other minds even when bodies are far apart. There is also a theory that when in solution, all the salts of the body can be made to crystallize into any desired shape by the concentrated effort of thought upon them. The result is spiritual materialization, and it is a rapidly escalating idea that after passing from his physical body, man can live and return to other spheres. The phenomenon we call a ghost is no longer something for science to scoff about. It is not unlikely that the "ghosts" of the ancient Atlanteans are around today, able to guide some people to seek all forms of ancient wisdom and helping what is popularly called the occult explosion.

The oldest known facts of religion were constant all the world over, and became the basis of present-day religious thought; there is no doubt that the early religions were closely linked with astrology and were not simply passing fantasies of a few isolated people. The former religion of the stars was, and still is, an attempt to explain immutable truths, and now the science of astrology is a tool readily available for those who wish to use it.

Most astrologers at work today accept astrology as a tool, conscious that the study of the planets in relation to their influences on all living things may, in time, give man a better idea of his place in the universe.

2

ASTROLOGY SCIENCE EDITOR OF HISTORY

Scientists and members of the church today show great concern that astrology has the ability to predict future events—an attitude which seems to be just about as illogical as anything can be. Within the Christian bible are thousands of predictions. Science itself, delving into the unknown just as the occult sciences do, predicts that certain causes will lead to certain effects. Prediction seems to be more respectable when it is in a religious context or is issued by a scientist who predicts that someday there will, indeed, be a cure for cancer.

Astrology becomes a special threat to the powers of religion and science because it goes into the realm of mathematical calculations, and the world is still not ready to accept the premise of the great Pythagoras that "all things are numbers." Over the last eight hundred years, of course, astrologers have invited opposition by seeking to present a valid mathematical science smothered, shrouded, and even distorted by mysticism. This led to laws being passed throughout the world linking astrology with clairvoyance and fortunetelling. In order to get around these laws (now so decadent as to be absurd), some astrologers today still prefer to work under the auspices of a church or foundation. However, the time is now ripe for astrologers to realize that there is no need to hide their science under the guise of mysticism. Nor does astrology need the pseudo-respectable image of being part of a church. It has achieved its own schism from religion and is now sufficiently mature to proceed into the Age of Aquarius as a pure science. If it does not take this route, many thousands of years of empirical and ancient knowledge will be doomed.

It is utter nonsense to condemn astrology's ability to predict events on a national and personal level. What a person does not know can hurt him. Man always benefits from knowledge, and when he makes a mistake such as transgressing the laws of the universe and nature, he pays for it; all mistakes, accidental or deliberate, have to be rectified. We see the truth of this when we observe the rape of the countryside. Even on a personal level, we have evidence every day that we have to be prepared for events; for example, we must file an income tax return on a certain day or take the consequences. Sensible people all accept the fact that they must plan for the future, and the more enlightened they are, the more capable are they in this planning process. Astrology merely provides an extra avenue for information upon which plans may be more realistically formulated and achieved. The student of astrology has a desire to know where he or she is going; the horoscope is a map which can help you reach your goal while limiting the amount of wandering you are likely to do if you become a pawn in the grip of your own free will.

Contrary to the usual charges thrown out by skeptics, all astrologers accept the fact that man does, indeed, have self-determination—and this seems to imply freedom which, in the modern-day idiom, is rapidly becoming only a pseudo-freedom. Astrology is not a fatalistic acceptance, any more than the constant use of free will is a means to perfect happiness. In time we may have to realize that only by working within the bounds of the disciplines of nature can we achieve anything like real freedom—mentally, physically, and spiritually. The role of the astrologer is to find the potential of the individual, or even of a nation, and to guide them without sitting in judgment, so that they can cooperate with all the circumstances in their lives to find their harmonious places in the universe.

Every being is a miniature universe, programmed to respond to certain causes which will lead to specific effects. Given the right conditions, a seed grows into a plant; it produces the means to reproduce itself, gains maturity, dies, and goes back to the earth where the process starts all over again. It will struggle to achieve the state of perfection which nature has programmed into its particular species. Man is no different from the plant, except that with his misuse of free will, he is inclined to make mistakes that prevent him from developing and expanding according to the way nature has programmed him. Everyone can take either a hard or a simple path through his life, but the wise ones begin to consider the means by which they can modify the impact of circumstances, and one lifetime is too short to proceed only on the theory of trial and error. We have learned to harness fire, earth, air, and water, and to contrive ways to use them without their injuring us. In the same way, men can use pressure which could overpower them to create channels to illuminate their minds, bodies, and spirits.

By studying the astrological factors involved and presented in a horoscope—or chart for living—you can learn to cope with your difficulties and succeed in achieving harmony in this lifetime. To what extent you are able to confront and resolve your difficulties is often the measure of your success; the wise person does not allow difficulties to be constantly transmuted into failure. If, through the predictive force of astrology, you can be warned in advance of these difficulties, how much easier it is for you to supersede them and get on with the business of finding life a joyous series of experiences!

Many of the more drastic events in life can be changed by the pre-knowledge of them, so man is certainly not a pawn of destiny if he studies astrology—although the irrevocable facts such as life and death are often beyond the power of man to elude. Common sense, too, is an invaluable attribute for any student of astrology, and with it he should have some interest in the great philosophical thoughts of the world so that he may use them in improving his own lifestyle. I get so tired of skeptics, who rarely have even a rudimentary knowledge of astrology, condemning it out of hand and implying that anyone remotely interested in the subject must be mentally defective. Such skeptics always point to a case of someone who would not dream of moving without first consulting his horoscope. In all my years of being an astrologer, I have never met anyone like this, although I realize that there are some people afraid of their own shadow. There are even religious fanatics who believe that they must not accept any responsibility in their lives without first having a personal message from God. Both attitudes are equally absurd, and the product of not only distorted thinking, but also abysmal ignorance.

Many people also think—erroneously—that astrology is a direct link with the behavioral sciences. The latter is generally a statistical operation applying to groups, while astrology seeks to find the special characteristics and influences of the individual. It is true that the twelve zodiacal signs represent twelve different lifestyles; but the individuals within each group differ in ways and manners especially important to each. People born in the United States are called Americans, and this is a group—but within the group are millions of individuals, each of whom is unique to himself.

Investigators into the natural sciences work on the premise that through the analysis of diverse factors, they will find the formulation of uniform patterns. Today we seem to be involved in a mad quest for averages, and to date no one has really found out anything about that lovable but mythical character, "the average man in the street." Science has an insane desire to generalize and bend the individual into any shape, with little or no attention to that mysterious intangible part of man known as his psyche. While the scientist requests constant research of interrelationships, the astrologer puzzles out the meaning of planetary relationships which make each individual unique.

As each planet moves in orderly procession in the heavens, it forms angles with other planets. We know for a fact that it is these inner relationships or aspects that determine outer behavior patterns. If it is within the inner relationships for a man to commit murder, then there are chances that he will, once a specific set of circumstances combine with his interior motivation. Even with this awareness that the individual is unique, astrology is still a valid science. Time plays an essential part in its analysis. Within the horoscope, based on the hour and minute of birth (plus the day, month, year, and place), the laws of both development and destruction can be clearly evaluated. Evolution and entropy both have a part in man's makeup, and can be explained only by the laws of synthesis—that is, of comparison—of attributes and deficiencies.

Just as the study of the horoscopes of human beings is fascinating, so is the study of the horoscopes of nations; from these a new vista of history looms up. From studying the horoscope of a nation or even a city, known events can be more readily understood. From the study of the progressed horoscope emerge events of the future. Astrology's seeming phenomenon of prediction is nothing more than a facile ability to make numerous calculations by which trends are found. Within the trends and cycles, it's not hard to discern the headlines of tomorrow's newspapers.

History is full of wars and rumors of them, of governments overthrown, of perished personalities whom future generations dub as heros or traitors. History is also full of the cataclysmic efforts of nature in her raw moods, which can be foreseen via the paper circle called a horoscope. To the student of mundane astrology—that is, astrology as pertaining to world events—there is nothing new under the Sun. As the planets move in their orderly procession in the heavens, they make angles with other planets in passing. Given enough time, the same forces always come back into effect for historical events to repeat themselves.

A classic example of this was the assassination of President John Kennedy—an irrevocable twenty-year recurrence of the Jupiter-Saturn conjunction in an earth sign. In the last 130 years, every time this dramatic conjunction has occurred, a President of the

United States elected during such a conjunction has died in office. It is too easy to dismiss this as coincidence, if we think of the word "coincidence" in its wrongful connotation as being concerned with chance. In actual fact, Webster's Dictionary defines it as: "the exact correspondence in position, a happening or agreeing in time, contemporaneousness, agreement in circumstance, character, etc., exact correspondence generally or a case of exact correspondence. . . ."

Both astronomers and astrologers agree that at specific times the Jupiter-Saturn conjunction does, indeed, take place. And from empirical as well as factual knowledge, we know that at this time, dramatic events take place associated with the heads of state. Astrologically, a conjunction is the time when two celestial bodies pass each other in the same degree in the zodiac. An aspect is the angular relationship between horoscopic indicators, and aspects are judged as favorable or unfavorable according to the nature of the planets concerned, the angles between them, and the number of degrees separating the two.

William H. Harrison held office as President at the time of a Jupiter-Saturn conjunction in the earth sign of Capricorn. Harrison died in 1841.

Abraham Lincoln was President during the Jupiter-Saturn conjunction in Virgo and was assassinated in 1865.

James A. Garfield held office during a Jupiter-Saturn conjunction in Taurus and was assassinated in 1881.

William McKinley went into his second term of office during a conjunction of Jupiter and Saturn in Capricorn, and he was assassinated in 1901.

Warren G. Harding was in office during the Jupiter-Saturn conjunction in Virgo, and died in office in 1923.

Franklin D. Roosevelt was elected to his third term of office during a Jupiter-Saturn conjunction in Taurus, and he died in office in 1945.

John F. Kennedy became President of the United States at the time of the Jupiter-Saturn conjunction in Capricorn.

Each aspect becomes a planetary pattern; it is the interpretation of these patterns, among other things, that contributes to a complete analysis of the horoscope. The circle of the zodiac contains 360 degrees. When the planetary positions are inserted into the horoscope, the exact placement is indicated by degrees, minutes, and seconds. Each of the zodiacal degrees for each planet has its own inherent meaning and symbolism. The Sun and Moon are really luminaries, but are included as two of the ten planets inserted in the horoscope. Each of the ten celestial bodies can be in any of the 360 degrees of the circle, so there are 3,600 possible placements of degrees whose meaning and symbolism must be studied by any astrology student.

For anyone who thinks that astrology is a haphazard science, the amount of permutations necessary for a basic knowledge of the subject runs into something like four million! To me, this suggests that astrology was not wantonly manufactured from thin air. A serious study which can take a lifetime to absorb thoroughly, astrology has a vocabulary and a grammar: the vocabulary is contained within the understanding of the planets within the signs, and the grammar is concerned with the planetary aspects within the zodiac and the analysis through understanding of these aspects. It is no wonder that astrology is as old as man himself, and that it has been in use for many thousands of years, each generation and race adding its own knowledge to the foundations laid in Atlantis.

Many people are at a total loss to understand and explain the real meaning of simple, everyday words. Take the words "day" and "year," for instance.

A day marks the period of the earth's rotation on its axis, whereas a year marks the period of the earth's revolution around the Sun. That is really very simple, but many people get bogged down with concise definitions of what a day or a year is!

It is even more difficult to grasp the importance of what astrologers call the "Great Year." This is a period of 25,800 years during which the poles of the earth's axis complete an imaginary circle in the sky. The Great Year is also divided into twelve Great Months, just as the regular calendar year is divided into twelve months—but each of the Great Months is of 2,150 years' duration. It is really this Great Month period to which we refer when we speak of the Age of Pisces, which we are emerging from, and the forthcoming Age of Aquarius. The Great Months are named after the constellations, but are eras of time, not areas of space.

Linked with the Great Months are the Precessional Epochs; that is the movement of the vernal equinox backwards along the ecliptic at the rate of about thirty degrees every 2,150 years of fifty seconds a year. These were discovered by Hipparchus, a Greek astronomer, about 134 B.C. At that time the signs and their constellations virtually coincided, but now they have moved apart so that the vernal point has slowly retrograded through the constellation of Pisces and is entering the latter part of Aquarius.

A constellation is a cluster of stars. The twelve constellations which are divisions of the heavens that appear in the ecliptical belt called the zodiac, have the same names but not the same locations as the twelve signs. When the Piscean Age was ushered in, it was unusual in that it started a whole new zodiacal Great Year of a new cycle of 25,800 years. Pluto is the planet ruling the transition from one cycle of 25,800 years and it is associated with regenerative forces—something of the quality of the mythical bird, the Phoenix, who consumes itself by fire in order to be born again. This analogy seems appropriate, since at the death of a Great Year a new one follows and brings into being a totally different lifestyle. In the last throes of a Great Year or a Great Month (that is, an Age), chaotic problems begin to be noticed such as we are now experiencing in social, moral, religious, and philosophic areas in all walks of life. When we begin to study the Great

Months—the Ages all named after constellations—it becomes easier to understand that man was civilized much earlier than science is willing to admit and that astrology was incorporated into the early religions. The symbols of the star religion have been handed down in the form of legend and myths, all capable of being associated with historical facts. The religion of the stars also links into the idea that astrology at some time must have been a science revealed by the people of Atlantis, rather than one which evolved naturally. For this reason, astrology is sometimes called "the divine science."

In studying the cycles which are so important to mundane astrology and the predictive power of astrology, it is also necessary to understand the various Ages of astrological reference, which we'll discuss in the next chapter.

3

THE GREAT AGES

The Age of Leo (Circa 11000–8850 B.C.)

This Age, when the ecliptic crossed the equator and fell into the constellation of Leo, was the Golden Age when man worshipped the Sun. It was the great solar period, during which the Atlantean civilization was at its apex. The most famous of American occultists is undoubtedly Edgar Cayce, who literally kicked us all into the occult explosion and new awareness of psychic phenomena. According to Cayce, the Atlanteans had discovered the secret of harnessing the power of the Sun by concentrating its rays through specially constructed crystals and using the energy for practical purposes—something many scientists today would like to do.

The Age of Leo was one of royal authority, when methods of government evolved. It was probably the time when great spiritual masters withdrew from the world and dissolved into history, to become known as Apollo, Hermes, Osiris, Vyasa, and Dionysus. Man had to assume a great deal of responsibility for his own life, but always under the guidance of the Sun-god. We know that some creative awareness must have come into the lives of those who lived in the Golden Age, since painting, sculpture, and architecture have been discovered in the legendary lost cities of the world which are revealed from time to time.

From Plato and numerous legends we learn that the Atlanteans had enough scientific acumen to know how to release the energies of the atom and start off on the path which was to lead to their own destruction. There could be a warning even in the legends: They tell of a great master race who used their power selfishly, upsetting the balance of nature until the elements rebelled and produced cataclysmic upheavals. One of Edgar Cayce's startling psychic revelations—too complete to be dismissed easily—relates to the idea that the Atlanteans, having discovered how to release the atom, found themselves with a problem on their hands. We too have the same problem, despite our scientists' assertion that the atom can be a means of peace. We all remember it mainly as the energy which released the horror of Hiroshima, when a mushroom-shaped cloud rose heavenward and sent numerous souls into a newly devised type of hell.

All overlapping periods of the Ages bring disruption

and chaos, but the transition from the fiery Sun-ruled Age of Leo to the watery Moon-ruled Age of Cancer was probably the most ferocious of all. In this time Atlantis disappeared, its end precipitated by the influence of the watery elements of the incoming Age of Cancer. Not only do legends describe this deluge, but both geological and archaeological records attest to the destruction. Scientifically, it is possible to understand that Atlantis disappeared by the uprise of the sea, caused by an enormous shift in the relationship of the Moon to the earth. It destroyed the Age of Royalty and the marvels of Atlantis, and ushered in the Age of Cancer.

The Age of Cancer (Circa 8850–6700 B.C.)

When the equinoctial point moved backward along the line of the ecliptic, the Age of Cancer saw the decline of royal personages and brought in an era associated with the common man. When we study the astrological signs, Cancer is still associated with the will of the people, its moods, emotions, and motivations. We must also consider again that the death of one age is a point of rebirth for another, a period of regeneration when new beginnings can be made. The dedication to the Sun ended. The sacred fires died down in the temples of the world and made way for the pantheon of the gods and a multitude of nature spirits. Along came Pan, the goat-footed mischievous god, the antithesis of royalty—and with him came an entirely new retinue of fauns, nymphs, dryads, and satyrs instead of the structured retinue of high priests and priestesses. A new dependence on Mother Earth started in the Age of Cancer, associated with fertility; this was a soothing antidote to the glories of Atlantis and the splendor of perfection sought, attained, then lost through the misappropriation of power.

During the Age of Cancer, the Sun-father god image died and made way for the Moon-mother goddess. It was the beginning of the matriarchal cycle in religion, in which the female was worshipped and led the religious rites. The family came into being as a unit, and there was a movement from caves and huts to more elaborate dwelling places. Compared with the golden splendor of the Age of Leo, the new age was one of austerity, in which an entirely new style of civilization was born. Within its auspices, men began to learn new skills and techniques. Works of art of this period are crude but always express the idea of woman as the leading figure of society, a necessary force in the fertility of the Age. It was a time for man to become aware that as a unit, and yet part of a whole, he must concentrate on the means of survival so that his family could exist and ultimately whole nations could survive.

The transition from the Age of Cancer to the Age of Gemini produced a new type of upheaval in which the human race began to turn to intellectual pursuits as a drastic change from his simply being content to survive on the products of the earth.

The Age of Gemini (Circa 6700–4550 B.C.)

In the zodiacal sign of Gemini we first associate the sexual act with an intangible called love. In the Age of Cancer, fertility was all-important. The mother goddess was the symbol associated with the bounty of the earth and the female as a vehicle to produce children. The Age of Gemini channeled in logic and reason, as well as an awareness that man's emotions are just as important as the assurance of survival. It was an age when people began to express themselves more freely and devise signs and symbols. The use of calendars and sundials came into being, and architecturally it was the age when the twin pillars of Jachin and Boaz appeared. Legends tell stories of famous pairs—Gog and Magog, Romulus and Remus, and Castor and Pollux. The priest emerged again as a leader, but now he began to play the role of the magician as well. Spells, incantations, and talismans were part of the religious ceremonies.

The wheel came into being and the correlation of the heavenly bodies was used to make maps for navigational purposes. The special skills of the Age of Gemini were ceramic-making and weaving, both demanding the dexterity of the hands, which even today we associate with those born under the sign of the heavenly twins.

Most important of all, concepts of good and evil were evolved, and man became aware of himself as a dual personality in which both forces could function.

It was an age of dexterity, manipulation, and the inspiration to create, but much of the fine old architectural work had to come from the next age. The Age of Gemini set seeds which grew as the fertile imagination of man developed—and they ripened in the Age of Taurus.

The Age of Taurus (Circa 4550–2400 B.C.)

This age, although predominately an agrarian period, was the age when man began to be aware that he could gather many personal possessions. Domesticated bulls and cows were not only possessions but also symbols of a new religious fervor. It was the custom to drink the blood of slaughtered bulls in order to gain power through mystical transference. In this we have the foreshadowing of the Christian sacrament of the Eucharist. The Taureans drank the blood of their bull-god, and the Christians drank wine which by mystical powers was converted into the blood of Christ.

Human sacrifices were also common, since man at this time was logical enough to reason that if his gods gave power to him, he also could give something to his god—and the most valuable thing he had was his own life or the life of another. The influence of the Age of Taurus can still be seen in the pseudo-religious fervor of bullfighting in Spain and Central America. Just as the opposing signs of the zodiac affect each other, so do the opposing influences of the Great Ages. In the zodiac, the sign of Taurus is opposed by Scorpio. Ireland, a Taurean country, is reputed to have cast out snakes, identified with the sign of Scorpio. But in the Scorpion country of Spain, the bull is ritualistically killed; thus both signs are balanced.

One important step of progress in the Age of Taurus was the discovery of copper, the symbolic metal of Venus, the ruling planet of the sign. Once copper was found and its value appreciated, an interest in metals as valuable possessions was inevitable, whereas in preceding ages the gold of the Aztecs and the Atlanteans was merely commodity to use as an expression of religious devotion. Metal money came into being, making it possible to establish trading, to accumulate wealth, and to buy and sell possessions. Acquisitiveness provoked perhaps the first awareness of jealousy and greed, and probably gave rise to the idea that money is the root of all evil. The Age of Taurus started the age of commerce on a very large scale. But the religious associations of the bull were doomed to make way for the Age of Aries, the time of the Golden Fleece and the golden calf.

Probably no other age brought into force so many of the less desirable elements in man, including greed and lust.

The Age of Aries (Circa 2400–250 B.C.)

The biblical springtime festival is the Passover, which describes the way in which the Sun literally passes over the ecliptic from the southerly to the northerly declination about March 21. The idea of blood sacrifice was a hangover from the Age of Taurus, but in the new age the bull was no longer an object for religious adoration. We know from the Old Testament that a lamb was slain at the time of Passover, and its blood splashed on the doorposts to identify a household as one of the "Chosen People." The wrath of the Lord, through plagues and other mishaps, would "pass-over" the house and not smite it. The Hebrew word for "to hover or protect" is *pesah* and the slaughtered animal was called the paschal lamb. It was no common animal; it was regarded as the Lamb of God, to be slain each year ever since "the foundation of the world." Every blood-stained pair of doorposts became the symbol of man's new entrance into life. The Christian religion was later to perpetuate the slaughter of the paschal lamb and coin the phrase "washed in the blood of the Lamb."

The lamb was not worshipped in the Age of Aries in the same sense as the Taureans worshipped the bull. It was the golden calf that was substituted for the bull. Moses, the biblical Law-giver, was angry when he saw his people bowing down to the golden calf after the sacrifice of the he-lamb had been instituted. Moses saw danger in the bowing down to the golden calf because of its association with the Egyptian religious cult of Apis, which the children of Israel were supposed to have abandoned after the Exodus. Even in Egypt, the religious worshipping of Apis the Bull was about to give way to the worship of Amen-Ra, the ram-headed Sun-god. But for most of the Age of Aries, the bull and the ram were accepted together as religious symbols.

The time was ripe for religious wars between the two cults, and through these wars the avarice of the Taurean Age found fulfillment in the Age of Aries. In one war, battering rams were made from tree trunks with the carved head of the ram at one end. "Ramparts" were constructed as an architectural embellishment as well as to serve the practical purpose of being a place where warlike Arians could look out and be warned of any approaching enemy. The copper of Venus was replaced by the iron of Mars, making warlike weapons much stronger and more potent. Yet at the same time, some of the benefits of Aries' opposing sign, Libra, were also in force, manifesting themselves through the giving of laws to the people by Moses, Manu, Hammurabi, and Solon. In the midst of warlike activities, the Old Testament prophets warned mankind to understand and abide by the spiritual laws of God.

In Greece in this period the beautiful Pallas Athene was said to have been born, fully armed, from the head of her father, Zeus. He is often shown wearing a helmet decorated with the horns of a ram. The Greek hero Jason and his Argonauts sought the Golden

Fleece, symbolizing the energetic exalted power of the Sun in Aries.

Previous ages were associated with royalty, priests, priestesses, and the establishment of the common man, but the Age of Aries was the age of heroes, bringing into force the qualities of independence, idealism, courage, and individualism. It was the age of the man in all his arrogant masculinity, programmed to win or to die gloriously in battles. Those who did not become heroes in their own right could be relied upon to inspire others by the example of their own courage and their qualities of leadership. Few women were destined to be heroines, for the Age of Aries was the period when women were regarded as possessions that could be plundered, raped, and disposed of with little concern. Despite the involvement with epics of valor, the heroes were unique in their individualism, leaving behind them few guidelines for the conduct of any great mass of people. The Age of Aries gave way, fighting valiantly to the last, to the more idealistic Age of Pisces.

The Age of Pisces (Circa 250 B.C.–A.D. 1900)

The Piscean Age started with the decline of the Greek civilization, some time before the actual birth of Christ. The dissolution of Rome was almost complete, despite the switching of the temporal power of the Roman Empire to the Church of Rome. Astrology was sufficiently well developed for people to realize that the conjunction of Mars, Jupiter, and Saturn in Pisces in the sixth century was the omen of the birth of a new god. The mystical areas of many religious cults began to be manifested as a balm to the terrifying brutality of the Age of Aries. A new word called "compassion" was to set the tempo for the new age. Governments that had previously oppressed and plundered others, finding their lesser counterpart in the lives of single individuals who took what they wanted by force, now changed to become considerate of the vast masses of destitute human beings. Religious and monastic orders began to appear, along with the first animal hospitals, including one founded in India in 250 B.C.

When man has been terribly oppressed and forced to live in fear of his life, he has a natural urge to flee—and the Piscean Age was the time when the first circumnavigation of the globe occurred. The warlike instinct did not die away immediately but now battles were fought on the oceans rather than on land. Many of the great cities of our time were built because of an increasing awareness that trade and commerce were linked with the waterways of the world. Pisces is a watery sign ruled jointly by Neptune, the trident-carrying ruler of the oceans, and Jupiter, the planet of expansion. The Taurean Age had respected the *earth,* and now it was time to utilize the great oceans and the waterways of the world as well as water itself for purposes other than drinking. As Virgo is the opposing sign to Pisces, the attributes of Virgo in the realms of general hygiene were brought into being, and bathing and scrubbing were more in evidence than ever before.

It is interesting to note when studying the Great Months—that is, the zodiacal ages—that the influences of the succeeding age and its corresponding sign are more in evidence in the first half of the Age; then in the latter half the influences of the opposing sign seem to take over. The Pisceans embarked on an idealistic religion featuring the birth of a son of God living on earth as a man, and the female figure again began to rise in religion in the figure of Mary, the saintly Mother of God. The growth of religious orders of all kinds flourished in the first half of the Age of Pisces, but then dwindled as the opposing sign of Virgo, emphasizing the service of the humble man, came in to influence it. The early monasteries and nunneries were as much places of medicine as sanctuaries of religion. With religion's dwindling influence, medicine moved into the realms of doctors and surgeons who began to work as professional temporal men, not necessarily attached to a place of religion. The full influence of the opposing sign of Virgo came in the eighteenth and nineteenth centuries, when great strides were made in medical hygiene. But Neptune, the ruling planet of Pisces, aided the progress in helping to bring about analgesic methods during surgery. Neptune, the planet of illusion, was well placed when gas lighting was introduced into the streets of many cities. Finally the idealistic, religiously oriented, compassionate beginnings of the Age of Pisces met head-on with Virgo reasoning, establishing a totally scientific materialism which we are now experiencing to the full.

The Age of Pisces is associated with poetry, pomp, and illusions which had to force issues between religion and science and pave the way to the Space Age as part of the new, much-publicized Age of Aquarius.

The Age of Aquarius (Circa 1900–4050)

Now mankind is escalating rapidly into the Age of Aquarius. Gone are the days when he worshipped with religious fervor the Sun, Moon, bloody lambs, golden calves, and crucified martyrs; the new god is likely to be created by science. The world has gone through an age when man mastered the earth and bred animals, when he conquered fire to utilize metals and forge the instruments of war. Many of the world's waterways have been explored, and if man has not conquered them, at least he has gained a good working knowledge of them.

The Age of Aquarius ushered in the Age of the Astronauts. Progress in every way has escalated so swiftly that it is difficult for the spiritual growth of man to keep pace with his physical and material growth. Uranus, the planet of change, dominates the scene, making mankind spin on his heels with the rapid rate of the inventions brought into being since the turn of the century. Many of these inventions, such as electricity, have greatly eased man's labors so that he need no longer feel like a beast of burden. But anyone not able to substitute spiritual and mental growth in place of hard work may find it hard to know what to do with more leisure.

Man has the freedom in most cases to plan his day without regard for the regulated hours of day and night. He can defy the sunrise and stay in bed if he is on a night shift, or prowl the night streets in search of adventure. Remember that each age has within it some reflection of its opposing sign in the zodiac, and the opposing sign of Aquarius is Leo, the royal lion. We can expect a new type of regal authoritative command to appear in the Age of Aquarius, and indeed, we have experienced the rapid rise of dictators in many parts of the world. This change will be gradual and reach its climax in A.D. 3000 when world dictatorship by one man is a possibility.

The Sun is in its detriment in Aquarius. The old Sun-gods are dead forever and man may have to look for god within himself. So much has been achieved in the preceding ages in terms of both man's creature comforts and his ability to destroy, that now one of the major interests of the Aquarian Age may well be not so much to understand life, as to get grips on death. In this age the technique of cryonics has been evolved, a method of freezing a body against the time when the new god, science, will decide to revive it. Science has devised faster and more wide-scale means of death, but the laboratories engaged in producing life in a test tube have not kept pace.

To date, the only inspiring thing about the Age of Aquarius is the space program, wherein man has proved that he can live for limited periods in an alien environment. But personally, I notice that reincarnation is no longer condemned as a mad theory embraced by a few, but is at least being considered by most thinkers everywhere. In time we may find that the true liberation of man will be the realization that his spirit is as important as his mind and body. This understanding will enable him to cope with the new balance of power—removed from the church to the realms of new types of government featuring a totalitarian, police-oriented society. It may also be a balm against both the encroachment of science into the life of the ordinary man and the advent of a highly computerized society which touches him from cradle to grave. The twelve basic lifestyles found in Aries through Pisces are already being fed into computers of government establishments, and the only private part of man left is his spirit—the indestructible link with the supreme being, the cumulative total of all the gods he has known in previous ages.

4

PLANETARY ASPECTS AND PAPER CIRCLES

If lines are drawn from the center of the earth to any two planets, an angle is formed. Astrologically, this angle is called an aspect. Just as verbs, nouns, and adjectives are the key to understanding grammar, so the various aspects give the clues to understanding astrology. The angles made between the planets in a chart are the clues which unravel the mysterious glyphs and enable a realistic story line to evolve through interpretation.

Some astrologers only use the major aspects—square, trine, conjunction, sextile, and opposition—in their interpretation. These work well enough in comparatively simple horoscopes, but in studying mundane events, it is best to have full knowledge of both major and minor aspects. Like astronomy, astrology has its own language, and the use of a good astrological dictionary is always helpful. An *orb* is the range of influence within which a planet or aspect operates (chart follows). Just as in the cusps (that is, the lines dividing the houses or signs) the characteristics of one sign will begin to merge with the next one, so in an orb or a cusp there is a period when the major influence of the aspect will grow to reach maximum impact and then decrease in power.

The less the degree of orb in the influence of the planets in aspect, the nearer the interpretations are to being exact and the more precise in the assessment of finer points.

Every influence of each aspect concerned in a planet has to be taken into consideration. The joint effect of two heavyweight planets in aspect will always last longer than aspects to two swiftly-moving planets.

An aspect not only unites two planets, but puts a special emphasis on the sign if it is a conjunction, or the triplicity if it is a trine, and on the quadruplicity if it is a square or opposition. *Where* the aspect takes place sets the scene for the action.

Planets coming together to form an aspect bring a blending of power, but besides the principle major aspects, there is always a back-up team of aspects which cause specific influences. No single aspect is wholly good or bad if there is a back-up team which can provide mitigating circumstances. Eminently capable people who do everything in a proper manner still need an aspect from Jupiter in order for their labors to be fully appreciated and beneficial. When an individual's horoscope has an abnormal number of aspects within it at a specific time, such as the progressed horoscopes of President Nixon and John Dean, there will always be many complex circumstances and much turbulence in his life. The more aspects, the longer the interpretation will take, and often the little-used influences of the sesquare and quintile need to be examined.

The empirical knowledge within interpretation is based on the ancient Pythagorean involvement with numbers, each number having a specific meaning —and as Pythagoras said, "All things are numbers." The 360 degrees in a circle, when divided by three and six, produce astrologically what we call the trine and sextile. Three is the number associated with Jupiter, the benevolent planet; six is the number associated with Venus, a planet of attractive influences at their best, including those associated with love and beauty. Therefore, through empirical research, we generally find that trines and sextiles are comparatively easy aspects.

If we divide the circle by four and eight, we get the square and semisquare, four being the number associated with Saturn, and eight the number associated with Mars. Both Mars and Saturn are heavy planets, exerting a hard influence; therefore the interpretation of these influences indicates tension or stress of some kind.

The charts of famous, successful people often show an abnormal amount of both squares and trines which, when interpreted, demonstrate that successful people are generally those who have been able to overcome difficulties emphasized by the squares and then coast along on the influences of the trines.

SYMBOL	*NAME*	*EXACT-NESS*	*ORB*	*MEANING*
☌	Conjunction	0	8	A blending of the combined power of the planets according to their nature.
☍	Opposition	180	8	Awareness of tension.
△	Trine	120	8	Generally considered an easy aspect, involving no strain or tension.
□	Square	90	8	Often stressful, but can be used as an abrasive aspect to energize and become constructive. Too much attention is given to the square as a malefic aspect. In mundane astrology a square can force positive action from a government or nation which could otherwise be ignored. A square always demands that some action be taken.

SYMBOL	*NAME*	*EXACT-NESS*	*ORB*	*MEANING*
∠	Semisquare	45	2	Brings difficulties into orbit and precipitates crises, but may pave the way toward the benefits of a trine.
⚹	Sextile	60	4	Weaker influences than a trine; passing pleasures or short surges of creativity; rewards for work.
⚺	Semisextile	30	2	Much the same as a sextile, but is weaker and can bring some stress. In a creative period, for instance, there could be a reward for work, but also some strain through tiredness. Can be a mixed blessing, but it is an aspect that one can do something about.
⚼	Sesqui-quadrate (sometimes called Sesquare)	135	2	This is a square plus half a square and is interpreted as difficult because it has not only the nature of a square but additional worries and problems. It is an exaggeration of all the influences of a regular square.

SYMBOL	*NAME*	*EXACT-NESS*	*ORB*	*MEANING*
⚻	Quincunx	150	2	Tension-ridden; often implies a forced relationship from which strain can result.
Q	Quintile	72	2	Little-used in personal horoscopes, but can be useful in mundane astrology, where mass as well as individual psychology plays a part. The quintile is associated with Mercury, and can be interpreted as either strengthening or weakening the mind. From the mind—that is, through thought—action generally follows, and the action of governments and people in authority is important.
BQ	Bioquintile	144	2	Similar to the quintile, but not so precise.

There are several other aspects found in charts: *The Grand Cross* occurs when four or more planets complete a four-cornered square which also forms two oppositions. This literally becomes a "cross to bear": a period of great burdensome troubles can be expected, but an astrologer always examines a chart to find areas which will compensate to a lesser or greater degree. The Grand Cross is often found in the horoscopes of new countries such as Israel, which has had many burdens to bear in its first twenty-five years of existence. The compensation comes through the sense of achievement felt by its people, brought about by good aspects to Jupiter and often to Mercury. In many of the newly formed African countries the same Grand Cross can be found, but not many of them have good aspects to Jupiter; consequently the period of growth is less apparent than in Israel.

The Cardinal Cross is formed by the cardinal signs of Aries, Cancer, Libra, and Capricorn. The pioneering, outgoing nature of Aries generally results in this cross indicating that a nation will surmount its troubles.

The Fixed Cross is a square or cross formed by the fixed signs Taurus, Leo, Scorpio, and Aquarius. It is more tiresome than the cardinal cross, since it implies that specific conscious action can expect repercussions giving a "you have made your bed, now lie on it" interpretation. Nations under dictators often have this cross, and a patient conditioning to circumstances is involved.

The Mutable Cross is formed by the mutable signs of Gemini, Virgo, Sagittarius, and Pisces. There is always some nervous tension and activity when the mutable cross appears in the horoscope of a country. There is a desire to adjust to prevailing conditions, but not with complete acceptance. It is a case of making do, or of grinning and bearing it, but always conscious that one day something can change for the better. A mutable cross can often be interpreted as a lull before the storm, a temporary alliance, a pseudo-peace, or even an armistice or period of truce.

Aspects are found by taking the Sun as the starting point, and then counting from it to all the other planets, making the appropriate glyph to indicate the type of aspect, if any. After the Sun, the Moon is taken as the starting point, and the same process goes on until all the planets have taken their turn as starting points.

Guides to the Various Planetary Aspects

Aspects of the *Sun* strengthen and liven up the personality, whether it is of an individual or a country. It is the nature which is affected.

Aspects of the *Moon* imply that the influences of the aspecting planet will be fully received by the Moon, which is the most receptive luminary of the heavens. Such aspects indicate fluctuations of existing conditions; vacillations will influence the making of decisions and upset the emotions.

Aspects of *Mercury* are often underestimated because of their ephemeral quality. Mercury is regarded as a neutral planet and it takes on the tempo of the planet aspecting it. The effect is almost always on the mentality and nervous system, so this can be a stressful aspect. When the mind and nervous system are upset, then accidents are more likely to happen.

Aspects of *Venus* cause the influences of the aspecting planet to become softer. The emotions are affected and aspects of Venus are responsible for changing relationships.

Aspects of *Mars* bring in lots of reinforcement, such as an increase of energy. The driving power of a person or country is modified according to the influence and basic characteristics of the planet aspecting it.

The aspects of *Jupiter* bring expansion into action, often bringing increased opportunities from which benefits can be derived, and also scope for creative and emotional activities. The propensity of a person or country to be happy is largely a matter for Jupiter and its aspects.

Conjunctions and oppositions between Jupiter and Saturn occur every twenty-one years, but the basic principles of these two planets are dynamically opposed. Jupiter's desire to expand is counteracted by Saturn's determination to cause restrictions.

Conjunctions and oppositions between Jupiter and Uranus occur every fourteen years, and often cause a break from conventions, increasing the desire for freedom. This influence can be very forceful, to the point of stress, and so this aspect can lead to revolution, which in turn can be peaceful or drastic.

Conjunctions and oppositions between Jupiter and Neptune occur every twelve and a half years. This aspect can cause false optimism, dreams which never mature into anything realistic. It affects all intangible issues of life, such as idealism, psychic awareness, escapism, foolishness—as well as susceptibility to drugs, poisons, gas, or anesthetics. It was during this aspect that some of the most beautiful French Impressionist paintings were created, typically expressing the dreamlike quality of even everyday happenings. This aspect enables a person or a country to go through life as if wearing rose-colored glasses.

A conjunction and opposition occur between Jupiter and Pluto roughly every twelve years. It signals a period of regeneration which can often, as in recent years, result in violence as a means of seeking freedom, but it rarely achieves such freedom.

Aspects to *Saturn* generally indicate some type of limitation according to the signs affected. At its best, such an aspect can make a normally untidy, unambitious person suddenly aware that he can be neat and can have some ambitions which he has not dared to think about. This aspect, however, can also bring about feelings of inadequacy.

The conjunction and opposition of Saturn to Uranus occur every ninety-one years, and this lengthy period is the reason why some people never really make much of their lives. The Saturn-Uranus aspect can embrace an entire lifetime, but it is also an aspect which enables practical plans and determination to go into action, and these two attributes can often defeat the worst influences of this aspect. It does not contribute a great deal to the happiness of a country.

Conjunctions and oppositions occur every thirty-five years between Saturn and Neptune. Impractical schemes come to nothing and scandals thrive, but this aspect can be good inasmuch as limitations through difficulties can be the catalyst to bring secret forces to the surface. It is likely to be a period in which a lot of dirty linen is washed in public, and in this it is more likely to be good for a country than for an individual.

Aspects between Saturn and Pluto are a rarity; they often occur as one Great Month succeeds another. Pluto comes along and literally blows up the stability of conservative old Saturn, sending into the world new ideas on just about everything. Pluto finds the Achilles' heel of the taskmaster planet and inflicts a mortal wound, breaking up both the best and the worst of the planetary influences. Peaceful but oppressed countries that suddenly flare up into revolution generally do so when Saturn is aspected by Pluto, enabling them to make a new start in lifestyles.

Any planet aspected by *Uranus*—the planet of sudden changes—becomes more dynamic and often quite explosive. The state of freedom and independence can be greatly modified or accentuated according to the aspecting planet. The conjunction and opposition to Neptune occur only every 121 years. The last trine was in orb from 1937 to 1941, and at the same time there was a Jupiter-Saturn conjunction. It helped to get half the world involved in a war, as the previous opposition did while in orb from 1905 to 1913. Two major world wars, the Korean and Vietnam wars, and the uneasiness between Israel and the Arabian states have left the world in a nervous, jittery state, probably because Uranus-inspired activity, flaring up constantly, was followed by typically Neptunian false optimism such as was seen after the signing of the peace agreement with Vietnam in 1973. Even peace can be uneasy as the strain of war when released brings into focus new problems of mass adjustment.

All aspects between the slower-moving planets will affect a whole generation, a nation, and history.

Aspects to the ascendant are generally of a personal nature, while those to the descendant affect others who are closely connected to the individual or country.

Aspects to the midheaven affect prestige, honor, authority, and career—and also affect the relationship to others in positions of authority. In a personal horoscope, aspects to the midheaven influence the relationship with the father; in a nation, the father image is affected.

Similarly, aspects to the nadir or lower heaven affect the domestic sphere and family connections, and influence the relationship with the mother.

These are only simple guidelines to the interpretation of aspects. The more horoscopes the astrologer studies, the more proficient he or she will be, and this applies to whatever type of horoscope is studied, genethliacal (the study of the small world of a human being) or mundane (the astrology of the world). The personal horoscope helps one to understand oneself, but no man is an island and so his own horoscope is linked with the horoscopes of the leaders of his country and their relationship to the rest of the world.

From the examination of many charts, it is possible to get a glimpse of the world as it will be in the future, as the news of today is recycled into the history of tomorrow.

5

PREVIEW OF THE AGE OF AQUARIUS

Predictions concerning our way of life in the Age of Aquarius are quite easy to ascertain as clues are gleaned from the aspects. As Aquarius trines Taurus, the sign associated with finances, it is likely that we shall live to see all metal money disappear—we are already experiencing the loss of gold and other precious metals—yet commerce and trading will go on. Aquarius trining Gemini will produce a massive new type of trading, just as metal money previously made beads obsolete. Money earned by labor is likely to be paid directly into banks, which will issue trading stamps and checks; many banks are already issuing their own credit cards, as are many of the established businesses of the world. This tendency will escalate as each year propels us into the Age of Aquarius. More and more types of identification are becoming required; together with fingerprinting, computers deal with instant data for verification of identities. As welfare checks increase, money is no longer an ideal motivation for work.

Attitudes toward sex are rapidly changing, affecting fashions in clothes, makeup, and hair styles. No longer is it possible to identify a woman because she has a dress, wears her hair long, or is elegantly groomed. The peacock cycle has already begun in men, who are much more extravagant in clothes than they have been for hundreds of years, and the unisex look is becoming more common. The naked body is no longer considered shameful, and with fewer clothes come fewer sex inhibitions. Love has always been an intangible emotion—and increasingly so today as Aquarius forms a square with Scorpio, the sign of sex, influenced by the energy of Mars and the psychological impact of Pluto on the subconscious.

Sex was once the driving force for man to propagate his species, and love was the balm that reduced its crudeness. Today sex is a spirited game. Despite many opinions to the contrary, stripping the body of clothes also strips away the cloying mystique once associated with it. The seriousness of sex is on the decrease, and maybe love will rush in and for once manifest itself as something more than the romantic dream that was so beloved of the poets of the Age of Pisces yet so full of the Neptunian influences of illusion and deceit. Love in the Age of Aquarius may well be much more honest than in the past. Homosexuality and lesbianism are no longer considered as social sicknesses by an increasing number of people.

Attitudes within the family are also changing as parents lose some of the power of authority over their offspring. Young people move away from the family more easily, making new lives for themselves with an independent and often defiant spirit that would never have been possible in the last dying gasps of the Age of Pisces. The Victorian parent has no more chance of surviving in the Age of Aquarius than the legendary heroes of the Age of Aries could have performed their feats in the preceding Age of Taurus. Each age fights the newness of the succeeding age and the result is always chaos and turmoil until a new generation is born more ready to accept its own particular age. Already the youthful parents of today have a more tolerant attitude toward their own children's defiance of tradition, orthodox religions and the authority of the established churches, and outmoded senses of the value of money. The conquest of space by the astronauts, the first new-style heroes of scientific achievement, did not prompt man to want to desert earth, but rather revitalized his ancient love of it to the extent that he is prepared to sacrifice no more of it to commerce.

The trine from Aquarius to Libra brings about changes in relationships of all kinds, as well as a big movement toward revising the legal system—which has been long overdue. We have already lived to see the slave laws repealed and some attempt to legislate against ethnic discrimination, but we are remarkably slow in making adequate legislation concerning the rights of women. This is a hangover from one of the major characteristics of the Age of Pisces, when woman was considered an appendage to her husband, a reflection of his personality. True, he was expected to provide for her to the best of his ability, but this philosophy changed drastically at the time of the great depression in 1929.

One of the most notable areas of progress in the Age of Aquarius will be the emancipation of the female. She is already aware that though the new age will be one of greater brotherhood among men, at the moment, domination and leadership is still essentially a male prerogative.

The rise of the Women's Liberation movement did not come as a surprise to astrologers; it was inevitable as part of the entire liberating movement which is revolutionizing the thinking of everyone in these early days of the age. The new freedom made its first feeble bleats with the Supreme Court decision of May 17, 1954, concerning racial integration. Neptune was in Libra at this time, a natural placement portending further action, and this came about through youth demonstrations. Neptune in Libra produced an insidious yet nebulous contagion among anyone who thought himself oppressed. The new strike for freedom went from race to war, to the draft, and finally to sex, all through the transit of Neptune through Libra from

October 4, 1942, until October 18, 1956. Most of the women active in liberation work have either Neptune in Virgo or Neptune in Libra in their own natal charts. In either sign, Neptune, the ruling planet of Pisces, drives the women toward compassion plus a deep insight into an individual's relationship with her universe. It also encourages her to want to take action in order to rectify what she believes to be an undesirable situation. Neptune gives a psychic motivation, but unfortunately this planet is one with wayward, deceptive influences. Much of the action taken today by the Women's Liberation movement is unrealistic, although it does indeed spell out a vision of the future.

This lack of realism is also accentuated by leaders of the movement who have Uranus in either Gemini or Cancer, making them very versatile at best or totally irrational at worst. Uranus in Gemini and Cancer makes for sporadic demonstrations, which are as startling as shooting stars and just about as effective. In short, with these planetary patterns still in evidence, the lack of follow-up action accounts for the slowness of the movement and prevents it from being really effective. Uranus (the planet of the unexpected) in Gemini and Cancer (both signs concerned with dual personalities) exerts strong pressure, but often on the wrong areas of life. The peace-loving Cancerian is likely to be a militant fighter for peace, winning a battle or two but losing the war through lack of a back-up of logic and reasoning. Uranus is the ruling planet of Aquarius and very important in the new age;

it is certainly responsible for many women, such as Germaine Greer, being exceptionally brilliant in their professional sphere of life. It motivates reaction, but it is always impulsive action with ideas about reform as the target. Uranus in Cancer produces impatience and radicalism, both of which have been evident to date in the activities of the Women's Liberation movement, but neither Geminis nor Cancerians are very good at connecting their arrows with the target. The vision is distorted by the nebulous qualities of Neptune left over from the Age of Pisces.

Much of the dissidence among women both in and out of the movement stems from their awareness that they have been exploited because of their sex, and that men have a distorted image of womanhood. Dr. Sigmund Freud thought that this image began with the male's dependency as a child on his mother. This is very noticeable in young boys. Strangely, American mothers seem to wear the pants when a child is young and then forget his needs as an adolescent. The American male grows up insecure about his relationships with the female and the only time he can really exert his masculinity is through sex. After the great financial depression of 1929, many women took over the role of breadwinner and did it well, but destroyed the male image in his own home, and he has never quite recovered from it.

Before the coming of the Industrial Revolution (another Uranus-inspired phenomenon), the conflict between the sexes was subdued, although women have been exploited sexually since biblical days. Before the Industrial Revolution brought in machinery, few people had time to devote to emotional disturbances, since most of their energies went into providing for the bare necessities of life. Men, women, and children worked toward the common goal of survival. Today women do not feel the need to be bound to a man for purely economic reasons; the female has started doing "her own thing." She is in a better position to study and determine her own personal relationships, and she has been exposed to an educational process which teaches her the same skills that a man learns.

In this educational process, she has been encouraged to use her initiative, be independent, and compete with men in getting good grades. Then suddenly she is told that in order to acquire a husband, she must give up her initiative and her independence and never appear to be in competition with the male. After years of being programmed at school and college, she has a rude awakening in discovering that men and women are not equal. If she works, she must still be a good wife, mother, and lover, or others will think she is inferior; furthermore, the man has to be considered the breadwinner even if his wife earns more money than he does or is better at her job. With so much early indoctrination, followed by the contradictions which come when she goes out to earn a living, the last straw is reached when the girl is pressured by social conditions to feel that she is a failure if she does not get a husband. Sex inevitably becomes an issue for conflict and resulting emotional disturbances, and especially so for those with Neptune and Uranus strongly evident in their natal charts.

The failure seems to be not in the rebellion of woman against impossible odds, but in the educational system itself, which fails to teach that men and women are certainly not totally equal, but neither are they totally opposite. In a harmonious love—as distinct from sex—two people look outward in the same direction, knowing that each complements the other. Attitudes toward sex are going to be important as the Age of Aquarius gains momentum, and we need to get away from thinking that free love and sexual promiscuity are necessary for a woman who wishes to feel liberated—for real liberation is a state of mind as much as a physical expression. Neither sex needs to be in competition with the other, either professionally or sexually. Giving birth to a child is still an important function in the lives of most women, but being a father is equally important. Each parent has a specific role to fulfill when children are born.

The planetary patterns indicate that women will undoubtedly continue to seek liberation, and once the frenetic efforts to prove themselves better than the male have been eliminated, there is every chance that a new feeling will be established between the sexes. For some it will be in the form of an armistice, an uneasy peace, but a peace of sorts. The majority of women will find a new dimension in their lives as the role of childbearing is reduced with a regular lessening of the number of children born. The professional woman will become more liberated more quickly than other women, as employers rise to meet demands for equal pay for equal jobs. The next big upheaval in the liberation of women will be in 1985, when Neptune will again be in Libra; then a completely new revolution of the female role in society will take place. The muddled period of the 1970's will be a thing of the past, and a more realistic appraisal of women's needs will be in evidence.

One of the most important areas in which the new age will make its mark will be communication. This is influenced by the trine from Aquarius to Gemini, bringing into focus the need for an educational system that prepares the individual to cope with earning a living. There is likely to be a strong veering to technical and occupational schools where people are trained to work with their hands, understand computers, and use their minds. There will be greater ease in communicating with people in obscure parts of the globe, and the use of more and more satellites to connect country to country. Uranus is the planet that influences inventions of an electrical nature, and its influence will escalate. We can expect some startling inventions in 1974 and again in 1988, but unfortunately, many of the inventions will be of a warlike nature; also, many will be designed to help man enjoy his leisure.

Uranus was in Aquarius in 1912 from January 12 until September 4, and again from November 12, 1912, until March 31, 1919, then from August 17, 1919, to

January 21, 1920. During these periods unprecedented advances were made in radio, electronics, and aviation, all products of warlike activities since it was essential for armies on the move to remain in touch with each other. In 1913 Hans Geiger invented his instrument for measuring radioactivity in the atmosphere. In the same year Niels Bohr devised a new model for the atom which successfully accounted for the spectrum of hydrogen. In 1915 Professor Einstein produced his general theory of relativity, predicting the subsequently observed bending of light rays near the Sun. Meanwhile, the great industrialist Henry Ford perfected the assembly-line technique of conveyor belts in 1914, thus speeding up production in a way never before deemed possible. The Age of Aquarius is the age associated with group activities, and such activities started in the realms of industry. We are still subjected to pep talks by many employers urging the need for team spirit from employees, and in most cases people have responded, motivated by the appreciation that they could not survive without total cooperation. These ventures of Uranus in Aquarius at the turn of the century set the pace for the present-day involvement with radio, electronics, mass transit, aviation, atomic energy, and unfortunately many of the instruments of war. The transit from the Age of Pisces to the Age of Aquarius is gradually bringing about a more complete change in lifestyles than any other, except perhaps the age which brought the wheel into use.

Uranus, with its ability to cause the unexpected to happen, also upset old ideas about the arts, causing new departures in music, literature, and painting. Other ages produced what were believed to be miracles wrought by religion; the Age of Aquarius brings about miracles of science, and these miracles will increase from year to year.

We have just gone through a period of Uranus in Virgo, bringing about a revolution against inorganic foods—and fortunes to those who have invested in health food shops. During this transit we were alerted to the dangers of pollution and the need for more awareness of the ecological situation. Health clubs and diets have all been highlighted during this period, producing a wealth of new literature and a greater interest in health on the part of the individual. Large foundations have poured money into medical research, while death has become both a scientific study and a taboo word, and some people have gained a new interest in the possibilities of reincarnation. Uranus also rules astrology and occultism, and interest in these, too, has escalated, a phenomenon especially noticeable since 1969 when Uranus moved into Virgo.

In June of 1973 the President of the United States signed a pact with the U.S.S.R. limiting the use of war weapons, but sadly, Uranus in Aquarius can provide some false optimism to people in high places and generally cause the unexpected to happen. This is likely to result in a failure of the pact, and 1975–1976 will bring newspaper headlines indicating that the technical advances in drastic weapons of war have been insidiously maintained and increased—by both sides!

The transit of Uranus in Aquarius from 1912 to 1919 brought about the first Balkan War in 1912, followed by a second one in 1913—and by 1914 World War I engulfed Europe, the Middle East, and parts of Africa. In Russia, the Bolshevik Revolution in 1917 wrote some of the bloodiest pages in the history books of the world. It was as if the whole world was convulsed, a typical product of Uranus activity in which destruction must occur before new societies can be built up.

History repeats itself unless we learn something from its past lessons, and now may well be the time to sit down and do some homework if we are to avoid another war.

6

NEPTUNE PLANET OF VISION AND ILLUSION

Neptune takes fourteen years to transit through each sign of the zodiac, and it has a subtle effect on conditions, which change almost imperceptibly. It is both ephemeral and ethereal, dreamy, visionary and yet diffuse; whereas Venus, the planet of love and beauty, touches the outer feelings, Neptune touches the inner ones and has a great deal to do with the psyche. With Jupiter, it is the joint ruling planet of Pisces, the twelfth sign of the zodiac. Its influence on nations, however, often reveals the most notorious and nefarious mechanism, but of course its influences vary according to which house it is in. Since November 7, 1970, it has been in the second degree of Sagittarius.

Among its most notable achievements are the swing toward evangelism and a pseudo-religious feeling creeping into music and the arts. George Harrison, former member of the Beatles, produced a typically

Neptune-in-Sagittarius song in the best-selling "My Sweet Lord"; and as a modern passion play, *Jesus Christ Superstar* is a typically deceptive Neptunian ploy while transiting in the sign associated with religion and philosophical thought. When Neptune entered Sagittarius in 1970, it flipped the world into confusion in just about every realm. Some people thought that the new lifestyle of gospel music signified an increased awareness of religious values, and the same thought applied when newspapers reported thousands of people attending Billy Graham's evangelistic rallies. Fashion went berserk in a passionate battle between mini, midi, and maxi lengths versus pantaloons, pants, and tunics. Glamour was achieved either by putting on more clothes or by taking them off entirely and appearing in chain jewelry or provocative see-through blouses and shirts. The "Jesus freaks" appeared on street corners, stopping people and asking if they were saved or had been bathed in the blood of Christ. And if it was easier to say yes than to argue, then Neptune had another devious ruse to play around with.

Newspapers caught on to the seeming awareness of the new surge toward religion, but at the same time some pretty ghastly crimes were being committed and halos never really made it as popular headgear. Many records were broken in sports and speed trials, but Neptune kidded along, slyly urging more travel by air, then putting the skids on raising government funds for supersonic transport planes.

The worst effects of Neptune were felt on the financial scene—the dollar crisis in Europe in August 1971, and inflation forever gaining ground, with continual difficulties on Wall Street and the international monetary crises. When Neptune was in Scorpio, oil was the resource most likely to make a sharecropper into a millionaire, and those who did not make it in oil stood a chance of making a fortune by the sale of pornographic books, films, and magazines. Neptune began to gain momentum in its transit in Sagittarius, giving the first inclination that all was not well among the oil magnates of the world and slowly pushing toward an energy crisis—because Neptune's natural tendency is first to inflate and then deflate; it is a planet with something of the Indian giver about it. At the same time as the warnings went out that fuel would be scarce, the conscience of some legislators began to be concerned with the massive inflationary growth of pornography. But despite moralistic attitudes, there is little likelihood that there will be any really effective legislation toward burning pornography.

The biggest shock of all came with more and more priests and nuns leaving religious orders and not only renouncing their vows but getting married as well. Of course the erosion against the foundations of the church, especially the Catholic Church, began in Scorpio, the sign associated with sex. The Catholic Church is constantly being rocked by Neptune in Sagittarius, concerning such matters as abortion, divorce, drugs, and the revolt of the Netherlands branch of Catholicism.

Chaos also hit educational establishments, with riots at Jackson State College and with the Kent State University shootings on May 4, 1970, just one day after Neptune entered Sagittarius. It was a pivotal event, and such events are often ignored until historians have had a chance to take a long-range view in retrospect. Two such pivotal events in Russia were the firing on the peasant petitioners in front of the Winter Palace in January 1905, and the *Potemkin* mutiny later in the same year; we now know that these augured danger to the Romanov monarchy, that the events of 1905 foreshadowed the October Revolution in Russia in 1917. A careful consideration of the aspects in the chart set up for the Kent State riots gives a hint of tragic national disorders, fragmenting the United States as a nation.

On a brighter scale, Neptune in Sagittarius opened up a few closed doors in colleges and helped provide a wider range of subjects, which embraced courses on extrasensory perception, astrology, voodoo, and graphology. It also gave the first hint that certain countries were not excluding research into psychic phenomena, a noticeable example of which is Russia, providing a pleasant but typical Neptunian surprise. For who would have thought that Russia, the most materialistic and pragmatic of nations, had quietly been setting up research laboratories to study psychokinesis and other phenomena?

Photography is a special Neptunian pursuit, and great advances have been made in recording psychic phenomena on film; the first Kirlian photographs are now available of the subtle etheric emanations that surround all living things. Psychic healing is no longer a matter for derision, for science is finding evidence that certain people have magnetic fingertips and the etheric vibrations can be recorded in a completely scientific manner acceptable even to skeptics.

Neptune also influences gambling, and Sagittarians are exceptionally fond of all forms of it. Already there are moves being made to legalize gambling in New Jersey, New York, and Hawaii, and this will certainly come to pass during Neptune's sojourn in Sagittarius from 1970 until February 3, 1984. We shall probably have the first tangible evidence of this in 1975, when Hawaii is likely to beat New Jersey to the post. Meanwhile, Neptune in Sagittarius helps discreetly to disguise the fact that despite the legal connotations, gambling goes on very effectively in many places other than Las Vegas. More and more states are permitting state lotteries, overcoming the moral and religious objections by pointing out that such lotteries help pay taxes. They do, but they also act as catalysts for gambling on a much wider scale. At the moment, all religious fervor, morality, and interest in psychic phenomena are subjected to an enormous amount of theorizing and philosophizing, designed to elude the real issues that the Age of Aquarius will demand a more realistic and open approach to the things that people do in secret. But Neptune must disguise right to the last, so it will be in the last phases of its sojourn in Sagittarius when we can expect all controversial subjects to be treated realistically.

Laws are supposed to be made to protect society, but society also knows what it wants, and currently it seems to want to know more about the occult sciences. The law linking astrologers with charlatans, vagrants, and gypsies still exists, making the practice of astrology a crime in many states. Yet the public defies this law more and more as society recognizes its need for astrology and other occult sciences.

When we look back in history, we can see that Neptune has been associated with bondage and treachery. From 1862 to 1875 Neptune was in Aries; this was the era of Civil War profiteering, and Negroes began to know that freedom was something they had not been trained to understand. From 1875 to 1888 Neptune was in Taurus, and new territories were annexed to become states of the Union. Neptune transited in Gemini in 1888 until 1902, giving rise to a better postal service, a sudden increase of newspapers and newsprint of all kinds, and a spurt of interest in train and trolley car traveling. Neptune in Cancer from 1902 to 1915 brought a clutter of bric-a-brac into many American homes, in contrast to the starkness of the country homes of pioneer families. There was an inclination to gild every lily, with decoration running riot. One of the most important occurrences was the advent of the first home appliances such as vacuum cleaners, as well as automatic refrigeration to replace ice boxes. The Pure Foods Act was passed, and the family automobile started on its way to creating Neptunian fumes of pollution.

In 1915 Neptune entered Leo and stayed there until 1928—not a good position for the wayward, eccentric planet in the sign of the royal lion and the Sun. The sinking of the *Lusitania,* still regarded as one of the major sea tragedies, hurtled the United States into World War I. Woodrow Wilson made the first plea for a League of Nations and was defeated by Neptunian-inspired treacherous politicians.

Neptune played the same tricks with prohibition as it is now doing with gambling. Thus sprang up that unique phenomenon of American life, the speakeasy. It was illegal to sell and buy liquor, but everyone did it, and so prohibition bred its own type of adventurous buccaneer just as illegal gambling is doing today.

Leo is the sign associated with movie stars, acting, and the theater. With Neptune influencing photography, this was the era of lavish productions such as the Ziegfeld Follies and the lengthy biblical films. The financial world went into a downward spin and led to the crash of the stock market in 1929. Men who had nothing to live for when their material world was taken from them committed suicide.

Although Virgo is the sign of analysis and rational thinking, when Neptune transited it from September

1928 to February 1929, it contributed to the collapse of the stock market. But when Neptune again began to transit in Virgo from July 24, 1929, to October 3, 1942, it influenced the increased use of spray insecticides and chemical fertilizers, and vitamins started on their way to being a multimillion dollar business. Hitler did the greatest confidence job on a whole nation by convincing the Germans that they were a divine master race. Just as Neptune causes inflation in financial matters, it does the same for people, giving them illusions of grandeur. When World War II broke out, underground movements such as the *maquis* in France were as much in evidence as the treacherous Quisling groups, and the much-vaunted, seemingly indestructible Maginot Line proved to be nothing more than a Neptunian mirage. The British used the full force of their secret agents to infiltrate daringly right through enemy lines, while Generals Patton, Montgomery, and Rommel acted out roles of immense strategy to outwit each other in a "now you see him, now you don't" method of warfare.

From August 3, 1943, to December 23, 1955, Neptune transited in Libra, bringing its illusionary influence to work on the arts, while prostitution surfaced in unexpected places far removed from whorehouses and brought scandal to certain people in high places of authority. From 1956 until 1970 Neptune played hide and seek in and out of Libra and Scorpio, causing diabolical mayhem. Crime increased, and mugging became a new word in the dictionary, venereal disease increased, counterfeit geniuses upset the financial scene, kidnappings took place with alarming frequency, and the war in Vietnam was always covered with frightening Neptunian illusions and secrecy. No one quite knew if we were officially at war or not, and if they did, they were not really sure of the reason. If murder, rape, and mayhem were not enough, assassination cropped up, a blot on the national conscience, and to this day no one is really sure if the convicted assassins were indeed the only ones responsible.

Important areas of life seemed to be nothing more than a mirage, with the stock market dipping, inflation rising, some people suffering from overtaxation and others getting easy money from welfare organizations. If there is a strange realm of life which Neptune can influence, it jumps right in, scatters resources, creates havoc, appears to fade away, and then flares up again. The most noticeable example of this is the drug explosion in the United States. Despite severe laws against drugs, with vigilante groups in almost every city, the sale of drugs has burgeoned to fantastic proportions, overshadowing the government-sponsored programs for making nerve gases in enough quantities to put the entire world out of action for good.

During this time cheating in some sphere of life was a challenge which few could resist, whether it was innocent smuggling of one bottle of liquor or a million-dollar consignment of drugs. By the time Neptune begins to transit in Capricorn, the sign of law and order, we shall either have tidied up our world, smashed through illusions and deceitfulness, or made a new evaluation or acceptance of the fantasy world of Neptune. If we cannot face cleaning up our nation by ourselves, then the alternative may be that someone else will attempt to do so.

7

THE INFLUENCE OF PLUTO

In 1962 I predicted that when Pluto began to transit in Libra, China would be an important nation seeking friendship with the Western world. When I made this prediction, there seemed to be no way in which China would move from its insular position to form even a nodding acquaintance with the Western world. I also predicted that China would unleash its first atomic bomb, and was told by many important newsmen that China probably did not have an atomic bomb—but the blast took place. Well, Pluto began to transit in Libra in 1971, and President Nixon paid a visit to China and established trade pacts which brought a new Oriental look to fashions and an invasion of Chinese goods to stores across the country.

Naturally I was delighted to be right in my original prediction, but now I see some awesome implications affecting the entire world, and America in particular.

I do not believe that China has deep feelings of friendship for us; we are more than miles apart in ideology, but certainly China needs to update itself by using American technology. In return for our technical know-how we get Chinese acupuncture. Although we can be grateful for the opportunity to become more aware of this procedure, we should think of the price invoked by this exchange. American technology is the finest in the world, but it is also the one most geared to destruction. With the best will in the world, we cannot guarantee that the Chinese have only peace in their hearts as we send some of our best brains to help them update their industries. The year 1984 is the crucial year when we shall really know of China's true intentions toward us, and it may well turn out to be a case of biting the hand that fed it. Remember, we have offered a hand, but China will do the biting.

From 1983 to May 20, 1984, Pluto transits in Scorpio, its own sign, and at this time the world may be offered another diabolic bloodbath unless we work on the premise that to be forewarned is to be forearmed. The most powerful planets affecting the world today are the heavyweights called Uranus, Neptune, and Pluto. Of these, Pluto is probably the most drastic, for whatever it influences, the resulting action is irrevocable. The slower the speed of a planet, the more drastic and lasting are the results made by it in aspect to others, and it takes Pluto 288 years to make its complete transit of the zodiac. The aspects for the slowest moving planets—Jupiter, Saturn, Uranus,

Neptune and Pluto—have the greatest impact on the affairs of the world and when they are conjunct to each other, the effect can last for several centuries so that trends become well established.

Pluto is one of the planets which has an eccentric orbit, and so its progress through the zodiac is irregular. It takes thirteen years to go through some signs and thirty-two years to transit through others, but its average transiting time can be taken as twenty-four years. Therefore it can affect a whole generation to a larger extent than it can an individual.

Pluto was discovered in 1930, and astrologers are only now beginning to understand its influences, but already it has earned its name as the Dark Planet. Of course, the fact that Pluto was not discovered before 1930 does not mean that its influences were not felt before this date. It was discovered at a time when man was as much concerned with the intangible forces of life as the tangible. The Dark Planet is the outermost planet from the Sun, and the least conscious of that celestial planet's life-giving rays. It is the joint ruler with Mars in both Aries and Scorpio. Its basic functions affect the subconscious, spirituality, conscience, magic, occultism, and cosmic religions. In its more positive nature it influences the forces of regeneration, perpetuation, white magic, and many forms of power and ideals. In its negative aspects it influences criminality, the underworld, a general disregard for law and order, as well as indecency, the misuse of sex and occult forces, black magic, and degenerative and destructive forces. At its best it can alert man's consciousness, and at its worst it is destructive.

When we get cataclysms, earthquakes, landslides, extremes of weather, floods, and volcanic action, Pluto is there churning up a bit of extra astrological annoyance. It influences death, war, fanaticism, archaeology, prospecting for treasure and radium, and infernal industries dealing with iron and extremes of fire and coldness.

The great need for astrologers today is to understand the full impact of Pluto according to which sign it is transiting in. Since July 30, 1972, it has been in Libra and will remain there until November 20, 1983; then it will move into Scorpio, its own sign which it rules jointly with Mars. We know that Pluto is associated with death, destruction and war; Scorpio is the eighth house, which is also associated with death and regenerative forces, and this may be the period prophesized as the Armageddon. If we take a more optimistic view—and I do—Pluto in its own sign could also bring about great reformations in society and a chance for government funds to provide some much-needed financial support for investigations into psychic phenomena. It should also bring about some startling results in psychology. There is bound to be a period of purification and purgatory before the regenerative effects of Pluto in Scorpio manifest themselves. Sometimes we have to destroy in order to rebuild, but we must always be conscious that if we destroy we can build something better. Destruction for destruction's sake is never a good policy for a nation to follow.

It seems likely that during the years when Pluto is in Scorpio—1984 to 1995—we shall be made or broken as a nation, and it is at this time when man's own free will must be an important factor. We have the chance to guard against its being a point of no return, but a lot depends on how we handle the present situation while Pluto is in Libra, from 1971 through 1984. Its main impact will be sweeping changes in the legal codes of all nations, and we are about to embark on this stage in the United States. Since the scandalous Watergate affair, starting in June 1972, brought details of iniquitous legal matters to public attention, we have the chance to turn to a new, meaningful way of life by conscientiously tidying up the legal world. Once the law of a nation becomes suspect in the minds of its people, then a nation is set for decadence and ultimate degradation. The Watergate affair is a typical example of Pluto forcing subterranean matters up to the surface and giving us a chance to start a cleaning-up process, which is linked with regeneration. If we leave an open sewer exposed without attending to it, then we can expect drastic results, and the same principle applies to scandals and legalities. We have to do something about them or suffer from being exposed to them.

Libra is the sign of the balance, and Neptune transiting through it offers an opportunity to establish new values and new balances. But first the scales of justice rock a lot, creating a dizzying effect of chaos. The scales of justice symbolizing Libra are often depicted in the hands of a blindfolded figure. When Pluto rectifies the balance, then the blindfolds presumably will be removed. Today, with both Uranus and Pluto in Libra, we are faced with the chance to set the pace of the lives of the next generation. This is something of an awesome prospect but one which we should have the courage to face.

Another area in which Pluto's influence will be felt during its transit in Libra will be in reforms concerning marriage, birth control, and death—all issues that are attracting public and governmental attention at the moment. The scales of justice are taking a rocking on these issues also, as more and more states' abortion laws are being struck down and some states are issuing edicts on the "no fault" divorce. All these things, however, are only in the embryonic stage, and we can expect to hear much more about them between now and 1984—but 1980 should see abortion removed from any connotation of crime, no longer drawing rebuffs from religious groups. Easier divorce situations will come about much more swiftly; and by about 1976 it will be as easy to obtain a divorce as it is to get a marriage license.

We shall remain absorbed in seeing death as a taboo word for a much longer period, and euthanasia is not likely to be legal until the last few months of the Pluto-in-Libra transit, that is, about 1982. Note that free will is easily exercised in matters of marriage and divorce, whereas it has its minimum power in the areas of life and death—and it is in these last two areas that Plutonian influences have to struggle to take effect.

The conjunctions of Pluto with other heavyweight planets are very important, since such conjunctions remain in effect for several years. The major conjunction is the one between Pluto and Neptune, which stays within orb for ten years, with long-lasting effects for several centuries. The last such conjunction took place between 1890 and 1894 in six to ten degrees of Gemini, and it stayed within orb from 1887 through 1897. That conjunction brought socialism into being and had a direct effect on the economy of all nations. The results are still currently being felt in the United States in particular. Remember that Pluto has a long-standing effect on pioneering efforts, imminent justice, and massive upheavals affecting large masses of people. Neptune represents the influence on mysticism and all extremes, often leading people along paths of illusion and disillusion until they begin to employ careful discrimination. Neptune is like a misty day in San Francisco; we know there is some beautiful scenery to behold, but the true shapes and forms are distorted, and we have to wait for the mist to burn off before we see reality. The occult sciences are in the position of knowing they can do some good for mankind when they are understood, but we are ploughing through the mists and masses of pseudo-mysticism, waiting for the light of understanding to clear the vision of the mass of people.

A conjunction between Pluto and Uranus is also

important, and it remains in orb for five years. There was a conjunction which was exact several times from 1850 to 1853, in twenty-nine degrees of Aries to one degree in Taurus. The effect has been in force for about 120 years, bringing major devastating forces into the lives of many generations. The Industrial Revolution changed the lives of millions, with mass production and mass marketing, great reforms in agriculture, the acquisition of colonies, and the commercial exploitation of natural resources. The first oil well in the United States was drilled by Colonel Edwin Drake on August 27, 1859, and started a new age of economy in which oil still remains the king. It launched us into an area when materialism dominated spiritual qualities.

The next conjunction of Pluto and Uranus took place from 1964 to 1967 in fourteen to twenty degrees of Virgo. Mass automation escalated, bringing problems of unemployment, and there were strikes in the teaching profession which made headlines, as well as newspaper strikes which did not. An upheaval of social conditions highlighted the black people who struggled for equal rights, and there were battles between those who believed in integration and those who stood out for apartheid. Most dramatic of all was the sudden realization that large masses of people were taking tranquilizers, barbiturates, amphetamines, hallucinogens, and other mind-manipulating drugs. The Pluto and Uranus conjunct tripped off the widespread use of L.S.D., resulting in a new area of worry for parents.

We are still getting a lot of vestigial influence of hallucinatory drugs, but the worst is over, and the problem of drugs will begin to deteriorate by 1974 as Pluto transiting Virgo will alert people to taking better care of themselves and realizing that they have a responsibility to maintain their own good health. We are already becoming more conscious that natural organic food, good sanitation, and vitamins are necessary to boost health.

Pluto is the planet of self-destruction, but it also strives to unite the old with the new. However, the conjunction with Uranus, the planet of disturbances, will always first present a great general danger to humanity. Pluto conjunct to Uranus also affects the lives of politicians, breeding a lifestyle of corruption and underhanded methods, but the most positive effects of Pluto are to allow corruption to reach a saturation point and then to start cleaning up the mess. This is another example of Pluto causing destruction and then rebuilding on new, strong, well-prepared foundations.

The Pluto-Saturn conjunction is also an impressive one, staying in orb for several years and vitally manifesting its influence over the next thirty-three years. This conjunction took place in 1914-1915 and was repeated three times in two degrees of Cancer, bringing the United States into World War I. Pluto forces itself up from the nether regions, whether of the earth or the subconscious, and since Cancer is a water sign, the combination brought about the first extensive use of submarines. During World War I German submarines destroyed numerous cargo ships as well as the *Lusitania.* The next Pluto-Saturn conjunction took place in August 1947 in fourteen degrees of Leo, contributing to the rise and fall of governments all over the world and taking its toll on royal families, ejecting them from thrones with little hope of their ever regaining power. Its main influence, though, was on young people, who began to demand love and respect. A small revolution took place, and teenagers began to act like a race apart, with a common desire to see authority (parents) as a mutual enemy. There was an increase in leisure and amazing growth in the world of entertainment Television became a reality far beyond the dream of John Baird, its inventor. All the luxuries which once were the prerogative of the wealthy were now becoming available to everyone. It was the beginning of two and three cars in the garage, extra vacations, and a flurry of extravagance.

The next Pluto-Saturn conjunction will be in 1982-1983 in twenty-eight degrees of Libra, when the conflict of Pluto (demanding great upheaval) will be weighed against Saturn's desire to crystallize and retain the status quo. There is no doubt that this conjunction will affect politicians, and many heads will roll. It portends another political scandal of the same proportions as the Watergate affair, so perhaps we will not have learned a total lesson from the political chaos of today. At its best we should consider this conjunction as a second chance, when the last remnants of decadent laws stand a chance of being swept away—

but not without Saturn's putting up a good fight. Presumably we shall do only half a job of cleaning up the political and legal mess churned up by Watergate. But the wheels of the law move slowly, so it may well be that many legal reforms started now will only become a reality between 1982 and 1983. This also indicates how drastic the Watergate affair is, since it *cannot* be cleaned up immediately—even with the best intentions to do so. If we make only a half-hearted attempt at getting at the truth of the Watergate affair, then the effects of the next Pluto-Saturn conjunction will provide the major headlines for the newspapers in 1983.

Today's teenagers will be adult enough then to take an interest in political affairs and may well wonder what sort of inheritance we left them; perhaps this youthful spirit needs to exert itself to completely clean up political and legal matters. America *is* run largely by old men, and some of them have not grown wiser each year. The year 1983 will see another revolution —an even more ferocious battle between youth and age—and what youth will be battling for is the right to survive in a country which may well be on the brink of yet another war of unbelievable dimensions.

The Pluto-Jupiter conjunction is less drastic than the other Pluto conjunctions. It remains in orb for only two months, although its influence is felt for about thirteen years. Since Jupiter moves more swiftly than the other heavyweight planets, more conjunctions take place, and the following conjunctions are relevant to the twentieth century:

1906—in 23 degrees of Gemini
1918—in 6 degrees of Cancer
1930 to 1931—in 20 degrees of Cancer
1943—in 7 degrees of Leo
1955 to 1956—in 28 degrees of Leo
1968—in 24 degrees of Virgo
1981—in 24 degrees of Libra
1994—in 0 degrees of Sagittarius

Jupiter is the planet of expansion, often considered one of the most benefic planets in the horoscope (just as Saturn is considered one of the most malefic). Actually, no planet is wholly good or wholly evil, and Jupiter's desire to expand can be something of a boomerang. We are perhaps too apt to see expansion as beneficial, but often the expansion of Jupiter is connected with obesity or sickness. Remember, too, that the sign in which Jupiter appears must also be taken into consideration.

In 1906 this conjunction in Gemini added transport and communications, helping in the expansion of automobile and air travel, and aiding communication by the invention of the telephone and phonograph. At the same time, this conjunction started off a great interest in psychology—the ability to probe into the depths of the mind and the subconscious. The word "schizophrenia" began to have a new meaning. Man was approaching the dividing line between the Age of Pisces and the Age of Aquarius.

In 1918 man was again left cliff-hanging, looking

back on the most deadly war the world had ever known—and yet forced to look forward, with more optimism than he really felt, to a world which would never again commit the same crime. He was still in a state of personal confusion in 1931, but was intent on establishing himself in his own home, and mortgage companies were wooing him to invest in them instead of paying rent to the landlord.

In 1943 man was experiencing a backlash and complete bewilderment that war was again not only possible but a reality, and the clashes of power affected all the nations of the civilized world. In 1955 he was involved in a power struggle in his own family life, being shaken through the new independence of children. In 1968 he faced drugs and became aware that chemicals were upsetting the balance of nature.

What will we find when the Pluto-Jupiter conjunction takes place in twenty-four degrees of Libra in 1981? Most likely man will be in the same position as his grandfather was in World War I and his father in World War II. For he will be subjected to rumors of war and the knowledge that man's technology has reached a peak enabling whole nations to be destroyed in one hour of atomic warfare.

The picture changes very drastically when Pluto and Jupiter become conjunct in Sagittarius in January 1995, for then Jupiter can show its best side in its own sign. It can expand philosophy and new areas of spiritual awareness, and for once the age-old idea of Jupiter as a benefic planet is more likely to be obvious.

Man will see readjustments in trading and a decrease in use of metal money, but he will also see a decline in family life reminiscent of the days from 1943 to 1956, as well as a new spate of colonization which is likely to be connected with space travel. Remember that Sagittarius is the sign associated with long-distance travel; with Pluto and Jupiter conjunct in this sign, man will find it easy to go around the world in new types of planes, and the first interplanetary travel systems will come into being. The Age of Aquarius will be going full speed ahead in just about everything, and as the possessiveness of family life dwindles, man's awareness of his need for other men will awaken a new spirit of compassionate brotherhood which is the reward for those who live through to the turn of the century.

The Age of Pisces will be just another chapter in the history book, except that it will be appropriate to the times by being available only on microfilm.

8

KNOW YOUR ENEMIES

In 1973 the nation was hit with the scandal of the Watergate affair. Politicians who had once worked together and been friends suddenly emerged as enemies in an effort to save their own skins or create trouble for the Chief Executive, Richard M. Nixon. At the end of June over half the population thought the President was cognizant of all the details concerning Watergate. Others thought that his former chief counsel, John Dean, was either a hero or the archenemy of the President.

Suspecting that we have enemies is one thing; *knowing* that we have them enables us to deal with them much more effectively by being careful of anything they are involved in. Astrology provides some straightforward guidelines to knowing enemies; it often necessitates making up a series of charts, first for oneself, then for others who are in close contact.

The major consideration in assessing a chart for enemies is an appraisal of the rulers of the fourth, seventh, eighth, and twelfth houses—and then discovering which planets are in these houses. First of all, though, we must thoroughly understand what each house signifies.

The first house is associated with the personality, its initiative and field of action. It indicates what character we can expect to find and what the individual's outlook on life is. The first house is a spyglass from which we peer into the other areas of the chart. It shows the physical characteristics of the individual and his early childhood.

The second house is associated with possessions, not only material ones but also those affecting the sense of values. It shows earned income, finances and worldly resources, the desire to possess material things, and in general the basic financial and psychological security of the subject.

The third house is the house of environment, including brothers, sisters, blood relatives, and neighbors. It also indicates short journeys, education, perception, speech and other areas of communications, as well as intellectual pursuits.

The fourth house is the house of operations, the individual's home and the house of the parents. It also includes the area of heredity. Family and racial traditions are here. This house has special connotations regarding the subject's attitude toward his or her mother. Early subconscious conditioning can be found here, and the end of life.

The fifth house is the field of personal expression and of offspring. It indicates pleasures, artistic creation and capability, speculations, romances, talents, and "brain children." It is a mistake to think that only material offspring are contained in this house; today it is increasingly evident that brain children relate also to the field of personal expression.

The sixth house is concerned with service of all kinds, as well as work and health factors, diet, hygiene, sanitation, small animals, and everyday responsibilities.

The seventh house is concerned with the field of relationships, both romantic or business ones—cooperation to a positive or negative degree, marriages and divorces, legal contracts and legal trials, social consciousness, and adversaries.

The eighth house is the house of renewal and regeneration, the house of investments, deaths, and legacies, and all processes of elimination. The partner's resources show up here, as do sexual instincts, inheritances, and insurance.

The ninth house is the house of long journeys where goals and planning may be involved. In this house are senses of purpose, deep mental interests, and research; the search for new horizons, mentally, physically and emotionally; residence in a foreign land and involvement with foreigners; philosophy, religion, prophecy, publicity, organized sports and sports in which teams are involved, and also education.

The tenth house is the house of worldly attainment, positions of authority, prestige, and honor; also the potential for a profession, fame or lack of it, the influence of the male parent, affairs of state, corporations and large-scale organizations.

The eleventh house is the house of hopes and wishes, as well as friendships in the sense of detached relationships. This house is associated with all spheres of interest in business matters, altruism, and the rewards the subject can expect from the tenth house. Here also are group activities, including humanitarian and philanthropic ones.

The twelfth house is the house of hidden causes and behind-the-scene happenings, repressions, neuroses, and psychosomatic illnesses; deception, secrets, treachery, hidden enemies; restrictive institutions such as prisons, mental homes, hospitals; occultism; restriction on freedom of any kind.

The rulers of the fourth (Moon), seventh (Venus), eighth (Pluto and Mars), and twelfth (Jupiter and Neptune) houses have to be taken into consideration together with the planets in these houses. These are the naturally significant houses, dealing with the base of operations (fourth), cooperation or lack of it (seventh), elimination and partner's resources (eighth), and hidden enemies (twelfth). An afflicted planet is one which is part of an aspect of stress, such as a square, semisquare or a sesquare. Planets afflicting the Sun, Moon, or ascendant and the houses they occupy will show the source where loss or trouble may come from.

For instance, afflicted planets, causing one stress through aspects such as the square, semisquare or sesquare, in the seventh house opposing the ascendant show that there will be strife from people whose interests are different from the subject of the horoscope. Uranus in the seventh house indicates public rivals, Saturn indicates deceitful friends, Mars shows the possibility of violence, and the Sun indicates open and powerful enemies. Mercury in this house denotes commercial rivals and fraudulent motivations.

If Neptune is found in the seventh house, secret maneuverings, behind-the-scenes activities, and infamous plotting will go on to injure the subject of the horoscope. A badly aspected Pluto in the seventh house indicates an enemy in public life. It is also likely that enemies will use harmful tactics toward the marriage of the subject or his business partner. Everything is likely to be done to involve him in some scandal of a social, moral, financial, or business nature. Pluto can be devastating to anyone in this position.

Every planet has a negative or indirect connection with the sign opposing the sign it rules, and this position is called the "detriment." A planet's being in its detriment does not make it weak; rather, its power works in a manner contrary to its sign. The militant nature of Mars, for instance, is difficult to express when Mars is in either Taurus or Libra, both ruled by Venus, a planet of more gentle characteristics.

The following table shows in simplified form the varying energies of the planets (planetary dignities are the affinities between planets and signs):

PLANETARY DIGNITIES

Planet	*Sign Ruled*	*Detriment*	*Exaltation*	*Fall*
Sun	Leo	Aquarius	Aries	Libra
Moon	Cancer	Capricorn	Taurus	Scorpio
Mercury	Gemini Virgo	Sagittarius Pisces	Virgo	Pisces
Venus	Taurus Libra	Scorpio Aries	Pisces	Virgo
Mars	Aries Scorpio	Libra Taurus	Capricorn	Cancer
Jupiter	Sagittarius Pisces	Gemini Virgo	Cancer	Capricorn
Saturn	Capricorn	Cancer	Libra	Aries
Uranus	Aquarius	Leo	Scorpio	Taurus
Neptune	Pisces	Virgo	Cancer	Capricorn
Pluto	Scorpio	Taurus	Pisces	Virgo

A planet functions at its strongest in its own bailiwick; when it is in its detriment, it often shows some deeply rooted complexities, and a planet in its fall is restricted. When it is exalted, it becomes an exaggerated influence which can be carried to extremes, but an exalted planet also gives the key to its source of power and can often reveal a great deal about the inner resources of a person.

The sign in which a planet is in detriment is often called the "seventh house position," since this is always halfway around the zodiac, opposing the sign the planet naturally rules. Remember that the seventh house is where antagonists lurk, and it is also the house associated with partnerships. Compromises, the means of self-betrayal, and treachery by foes are also found here. A malefic planet in the fourth, seventh, eighth, or twelfth house in the sign of its detriment or fall, and afflicting the Sun or Moon, indicates a fierce enemy capable of being around for a long time and always with malicious intention. Mercury badly aspected by Mars produces scandal and slander. The same planet afflicted by Uranus produces quarrels, controversy, and lengthy legal disputes. When Mercury is afflicted by Saturn, it denotes treachery and deceitfulness, and when afflicted by Neptune, plots and frauds are around. Mercury badly aspected to Pluto indicates enemies who will attempt to bring a person down from a high position of authority, stopping at nothing to destroy his reputation by injurious and probably libelous statements. An indication of the birthday of persons likely to be enemies can be established by studying the longitude of the malefic planets in the horoscope. I have never found these to be wrong.

When the planets
In evil mixture, to disorder wander,
What plagues, and what portents, what mutiny.
What raging of the sea, shaking of the earth
Commotion of the winds. . . .

William Shakespeare

Richard Nixon was born on January 9, 1913, with his Sun in Capricorn and four planets heavily afflicted: the Moon, ruler of the fourth house; Mercury, ruler of the third and sixth houses; Mars, ruler of the first and eighth houses; and Pluto, joint ruler of the eighth house. He grew up to be essentially a public servant; all his greatest astrological conflicts occur in the tenth house, associated with his career, and all center around Pluto, the Dark Planet.

All the major afflictions in his life have come from the fourth house, from three planets in opposition, stemming from the area closely related to the most basic components of his life, such as prejudices and an especially narrow outlook. He is a Sun-in-Capricorn subject ruled by Saturn, and this Sun sign is known for its obstinacy and restricted vision. The strongest "easy" aspect in Mr. Nixon's chart comes from Saturn in the ninth house, influencing all aspects of foreign life. As President of the United States, he was by far the most traveled of any previous president, and he always seemed comfortable when dealing with foreign dignitaries.

A public servant with a narrow point of view is

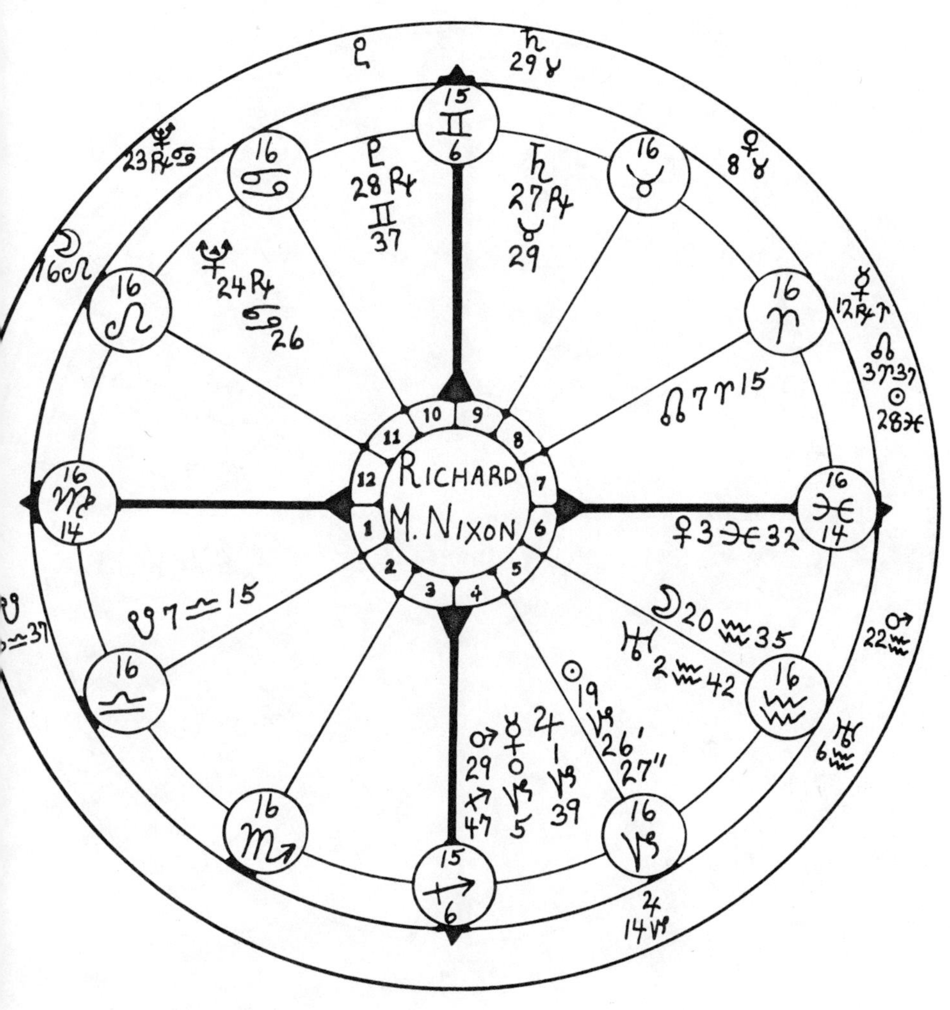

Figure 1. The natal horoscope of Richard M. Nixon.

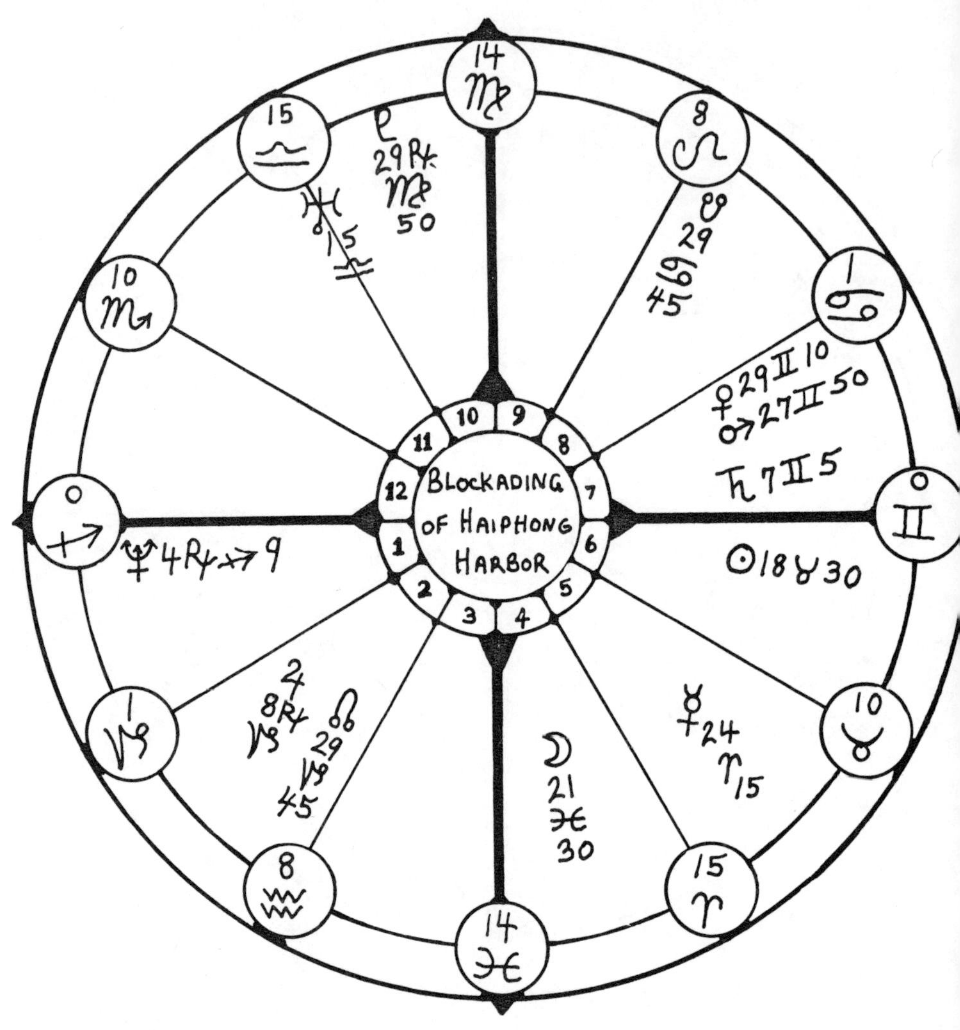

Figure 2. The planetary positions at the time of the blockading of Haiphong Harbor.

probably at a great disadvantage, because it makes him inflexible and incapable of dealing with anything beyond what he has established as a norm. Yet this same narrow point of view makes him act with his counselors for what he considers is best for the people of the United States.

The decline of Richard Nixon did not start with the Watergate affair, but with the decision to mine Haiphong Harbor on May 8, 1972. At this time the President's chart showed that he had no less than thirty-five major aspects churning around in it, and only two could be called moderately easy ones. With retrograde Neptune rising, opposite Saturn in the seventh house, the whole chart screams out that this is the beginning of a series of mistakes. The Saturn-Neptune opposition shows that a number of his supporters will leave his camp and shows rebellion from his advisors.

Pluto in the tenth house opposing the Moon in the fourth signifies concern and unexpected action by the public—but in the sphere of domestic activities, not the foreign ones, which would be more logical. The two planets were exerting opposition against Nixon's status quo in his role as President of the United States, but threatening the status quo of his personal life as well. All this was strengthened in its violence by the dangerous T-square to Venus and Mars. When planets in opposition to each other are squared by a third and focal planet, the configuration is called a T-square. Such a square focuses on the planet or planets which square the opposition and produce a vortex of force fields. The effect on a person is that he has to fight on two or more fronts at once and is often obliged to make concessions in an effort to compensate one front against the other. Maintaining a balanced view or even a consistent one is obviously difficult. The President's chart was in this T-square position in early May 1970, when the announcement of the Cambodian invasion resulted in widespread opposition which triggered off the tragedy of Kent State University. It took about six weeks for the miserable T-square to really make its presence known to the world. On May 8, 1972, noting the same T-square, an astrologer would know that within six weeks another world-shaking event would affect the life of the President. It came, three days short of six weeks, with the Watergate break-in on June 17, 1972.

Further long-range effects could be estimated by the Saturn-Neptune opposition and the inclusion of the drastic Pluto in the mutable T-square. May 8, 1972, was the beginning of dire afflictions in the President's life. When his birth chart was progressed to his birthday in 1972, no less than sixty stormy aspects were in his chart. Certainly a lot of activity could be expected in his life. Thirteen of these aspects were hitting his tenth house, which is associated with honor, prestige, and profession.

Strangely enough, John Dean, former chief counsel to the President, also had exactly sixty aspects after his natal chart was progressed. It is most unusual to prepare two charts, progress them, and find that *both*

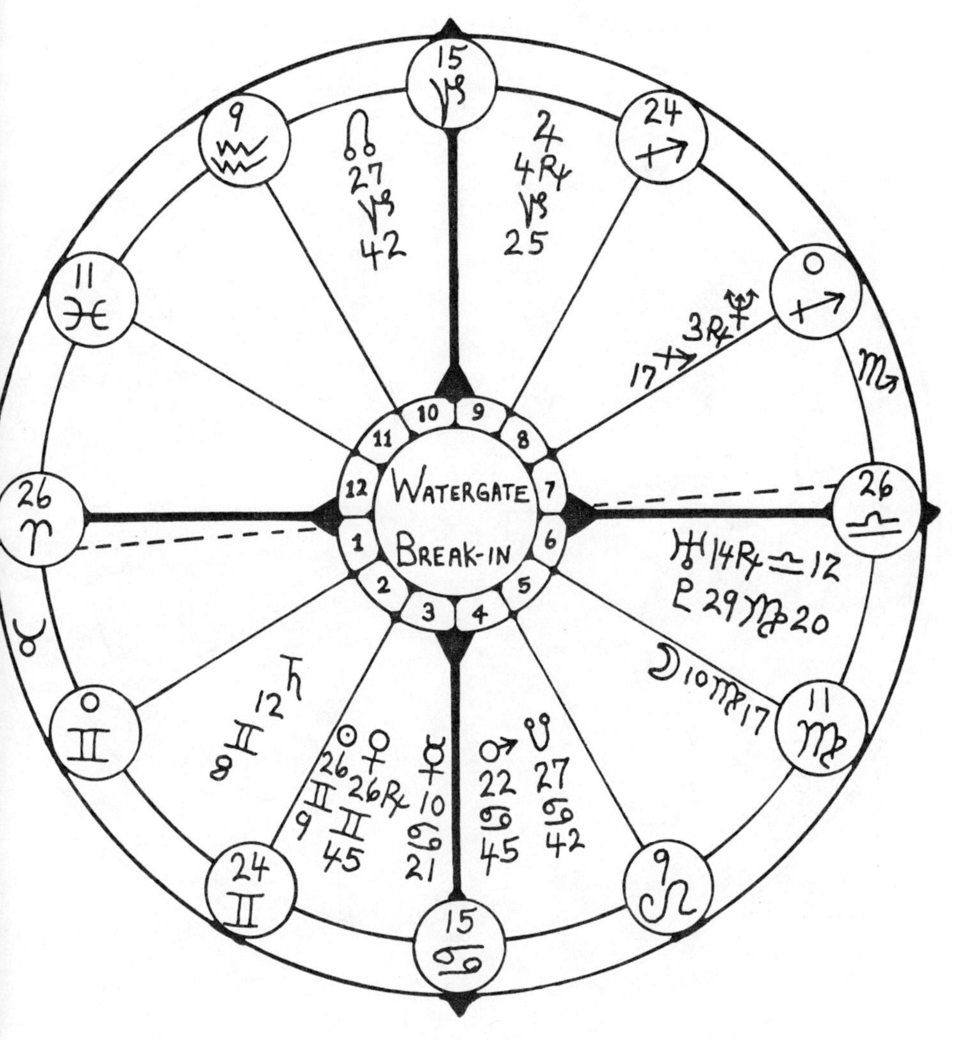

Figure 3. The planetary positions at the time of the Watergate break-in.

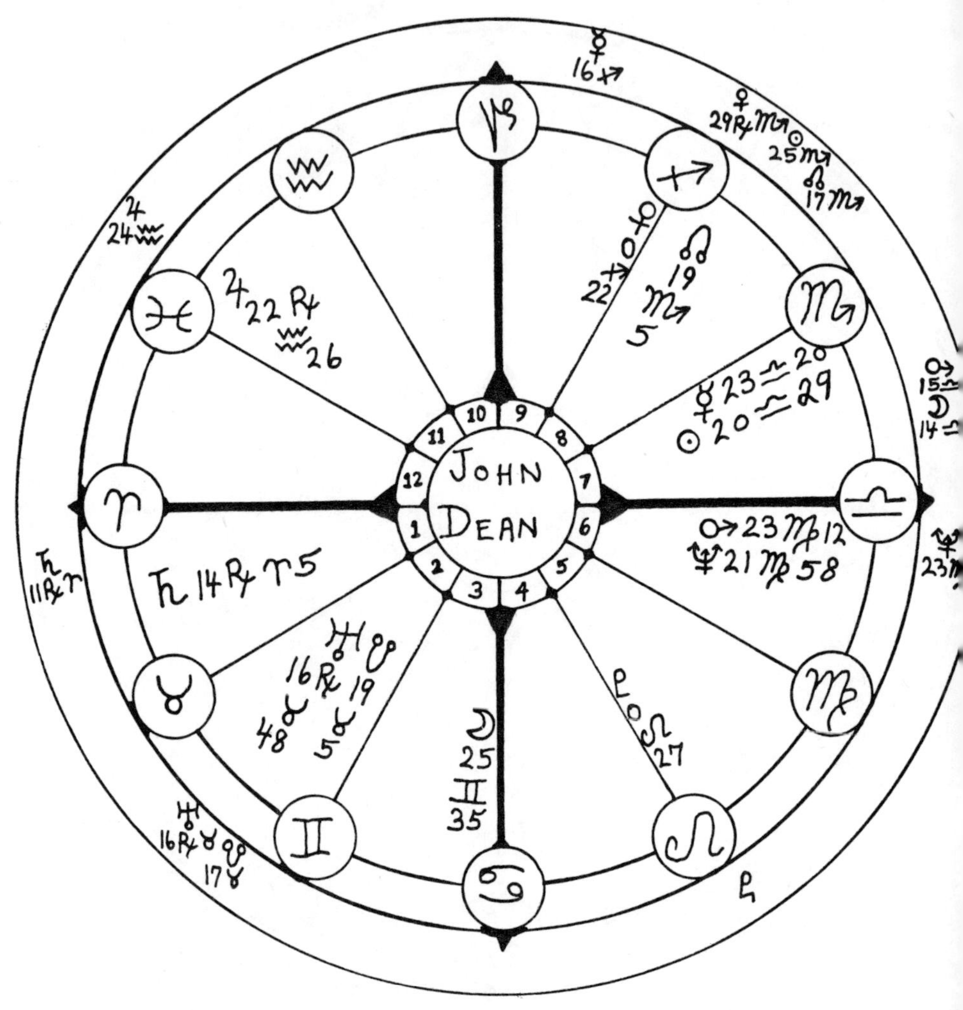

Figure 4. The natal horoscope of John Dean.

have exactly the same number of aspects within them. Mr. Dean had eight aspects mainly affecting his seventh and eighth houses, associated with enemies; one of these indicated that at some time during 1973 his life would be in mortal danger.

In the August 1972 issue of my magazine, *Astrology,* the following passages appeared. When reread almost a year later, they seem pertinent to the life and time of President Nixon.

> When a person with his Sun in Virgo or with Virgo ascendant is given a great many responsibilities (Mr. Nixon's ascendant is Virgo), they go to his head. When this happens to a Virgo, he "can't see the forest for the trees." That is to say, narrowness of view sets in and the goal is all that matters. Nixon, then, appears to associate himself personally with his established goals as President, and seems determined to reach them no matter what the cost. The crisis of control in its purest sense, then, is symbolized by the Pluto square between the first and tenth houses.
>
> The ego getting in the way of the job. It is an old story, sometimes related to us with a quizzical "Will success spoil . . . ?"
>
> Nixon brings to the Presidency the efficient talents of the civil servant or the bureaucrat, and a sense of his own destiny in service. The times, however, demand more boldness than that.

Since 1973 will be a year remembered in the annals of American history, students of astrology might like to study the aspects of the progressed chart of President Richard M. Nixon and that of his one-time chief counsel, Mr. John Dean. From an understanding of the aspects in any chart, the shadow of forthcoming national or personal events can be estimated. This is really what mundane astrology is all about.

PRESIDENT RICHARD M. NIXON

I. *Aspects from Sun*

1. Radical Sun in fifth house trine radical Saturn in ninth house.
2. Radical Sun in fifth house oppose radical Neptune in eleventh house.
3. Radical Sun in fifth house trine radical ascendant.
4. Radical Sun in fifth house square progressed Mercury in seventh house.
5. Radical Sun in fifth house conjunct progressed Jupiter in fourth house.
6. Radical Sun in fifth house oppose progressed Neptune in eleventh house.
7. Progressed Sun in seventh house sextile progressed Saturn in ninth house.
8. Progressed Sun in seventh house sextile progressed Uranus in fifth house.
9. Progressed Sun in seventh house trine progressed Neptune in eleventh house.
10. Progressed Sun in seventh house square progressed Pluto in tenth house.
11. Progressed Sun in seventh house conjunct progressed North Node and oppose progressed

South Node. The two points at which the plane of the Moon's orbit intersects the plane of the ecliptic are called "lunar nodes." The North Node shows where the Moon's path crosses the Sun's path from south to north. The South Node shows where the Moon passes from a northerly to a southerly celestial latitude.

II. *Aspects from Moon*

1. Radical Moon in sixth house sextile radical Mercury in fourth house.
2. Radical Moon in sixth house sextile radical Mars in fourth House.
3. Radical Moon in sixth house square radical Saturn in ninth house.
4. Radical Moon in sixth house trine radical Pluto in tenth house.
5. Radical Moon in sixth house trine radical midheaven.
6. Radical Moon in sixth house sextile progressed Mercury in seventh house.
7. Radical Moon in sixth house conjunct progressed Mars in sixth house.
8. Radical Moon in sixth house square progressed Saturn in ninth house.
9. Radical Moon in sixth house trine progressed Pluto in tenth house.
10. Progressed Moon on cusp of eleventh and twelfth houses trine progressed Mercury in seventh house.
11. Progressed Moon on cusp of eleventh and twelfth houses square progressed Venus in eighth house.
12. Progressed Moon on cusp of eleventh and

twelfth houses oppose progressed Mars in sixth house.

13. Progressed Moon on cusp of eleventh and twelfth houses oppose progressed Uranus in fifth house.

III. *Aspects from Mercury*

1. Radical Mercury in fourth house sextile radical Venus in sixth house.
2. Radical Mercury in fourth house conjunct radical Mars in fourth house.
3. Radical Mercury in fourth house conjunct radical Jupiter in fourth house.
4. Radical Mercury in fourth house oppose radical Pluto in tenth house.
5. Radical Mercury in fourth house oppose progressed Pluto in tenth house.
6. Radical Mercury in fourth house square progressed North Node and progressed South Node.
7. Progressed Mercury in seventh house square progressed Jupiter in fourth house.
8. Progressed Mercury in seventh house sextile progressed Uranus in fifth house.

IV. *Aspects from Venus*

1. Radical Venus in sixth house sextile radical Mars in fourth house.
2. Radical Venus in sixth house sextile radical Jupiter in fourth house.
3. Radical Venus in sixth house square radical Saturn in ninth house.
4. Radical Venus in sixth house trine radical Pluto in tenth house.
5. Radical Venus in sixth house square progressed Saturn in ninth house.

6. Radical Venus in sixth house trine progressed Pluto in tenth house.
7. Progressed Venus in eighth house trine progressed Jupiter in fourth house.
8. Progressed Venus in eighth house square progressed Uranus in fifth house.

V. *Aspects from Mars*

1. Radical Mars in fourth house conjunct radical Jupiter in fourth house.
2. Radical Mars in fourth house oppose radical Pluto in tenth house.
3. Radical Mars in fourth house oppose progressed Pluto in tenth house.
4. Radical Mars in fourth house square progressed North Node and progressed South Node.
5. Progressed Mars in sixth house trine progressed Pluto in tenth house.

VI. *Aspects from Jupiter*

1. Radical Jupiter in fourth house oppose radical Pluto in tenth house.
2. Radical Jupiter in fourth house square radical North Node and radical South Node.
3. Radical Jupiter in fourth house oppose progressed Pluto in tenth house.
4. Radical Jupiter in fourth house square progressed North Node and progressed South Node.

VII. *Aspects from Saturn*

1. Radical Saturn in ninth house trine radical Uranus in fifth house.
2. Radical Saturn in ninth house sextile radical Neptune in eleventh house.

3. Radical Saturn in ninth house sextile progressed Neptune in eleventh house.
4. Radical Saturn in ninth house sextile progressed North Node and trine progressed South Node.
5. Progressed Saturn in ninth house sextile progressed Neptune in eleventh house.
6. Progressed Saturn in ninth house sextile progressed North Node and trine progressed South Node.

VIII. *Aspects from Uranus*

1. Radical Uranus in fifth house sextile radical North Node and trine radical South Node.
2. Radical Uranus in fifth house sextile progressed North Node and trine progressed South Node.
3. Progressed Uranus in fifth house sextile progressed North Node and trine progressed South Node.

IX. *Aspects from Pluto*

1. Radical Pluto in tenth house square progressed North Node and progressed South Node.
2. Progressed Pluto in tenth house square progressed North Node and progressed South Node.

JOHN DEAN

I. *Aspects from Sun*

1. Radical Sun in seventh house trine radical Moon in third house.
2. Radical Sun in seventh house conjunct radical Mercury in seventh house.
3. Radical Sun in seventh house trine radical Jupiter in eleventh house.

4. Radical Sun in seventh house oppose radical Saturn in first house.
5. Radical Sun in seventh house conjunct progressed Moon in seventh house.
6. Radical Sun in seventh house sextile progressed Mercury in ninth house.
7. Radical Sun in seventh house conjunct progressed Mars in seventh house.
8. Radical Sun in seventh house trine progressed Jupiter in eleventh house.
9. Radical Sun in seventh house oppose progressed Saturn in first house.
10. Progressed Sun in eighth house conjunct progressed Venus in eighth house.
11. Progressed Sun in eighth house square progressed Jupiter in eleventh house.
12. Progressed Sun in eighth house oppose progressed Uranus in second house.
13. Progressed Sun in eighth house sextile progressed Neptune in sixth house.
14. Progressed Sun in eighth house trine progressed Pluto in fifth house.
15. Progressed Sun in eighth house conjunct progressed North Node and oppose progressed South Node.

II. *Aspects from Moon*

1. Radical Moon in third house trine radical Mercury in seventh house.
2. Radical Moon in third house square radical Mars in sixth house.
3. Radical Moon in third house trine radical Jupiter in eleventh house.
4. Radical Moon in third house square radical Neptune in sixth house.

5. Radical Moon in third house oppose progressed Mercury in ninth house.
6. Radical Moon in third house trine progressed Mars in seventh house.
7. Radical Moon in third house trine progressed Jupiter in eleventh house.
8. Radical Moon in third house square progressed Neptune in sixth house.
9. Progressed Moon in seventh house sextile progressed Mercury in ninth house.
10. Progressed Moon in seventh house conjunct progressed Mars in seventh house.
11. Progressed Moon in seventh house trine progressed Jupiter in eleventh house.
12. Progressed Moon in seventh house oppose progressed Saturn in first house.

III. *Aspects from Mercury*

1. Radical Mercury in seventh house trine radical Jupiter in eleventh house.
2. Radical Mercury in seventh house trine progressed Jupiter in eleventh house.
3. Progressed Mercury in ninth house sextile progressed Mars in seventh house.
4. Progressed Mercury in ninth house trine progressed Saturn in first house.
5. Progressed Mercury in ninth house square progressed Neptune in sixth house.

IV. *Aspects from Venus*

1. Radical Venus in ninth house trine radical Pluto in fifth house.
2. Radical Venus in ninth house square progressed Jupiter in eleventh house.

3. Radical Venus in ninth house trine progressed Pluto in fifth house.
4. Progressed Venus in eighth house square progressed Jupiter in eleventh house.
5. Progressed Venus in eighth house sextile progressed Neptune in sixth house.
6. Progressed Venus in eighth house trine progressed Pluto in fifth house.

V. *Aspects from Mars*

1. Radical Mars in sixth house trine radical Uranus in second house.
2. Radical Mars in sixth house conjunct radical Neptune in sixth house.
3. Radical Mars in sixth house sextile radical North Node and trine radical South Node.
4. Radical Mars in sixth house trine progressed Uranus in second house.
5. Radical Mars in sixth house exact conjunction with progressed Neptune in sixth house.
6. Radical Mars in sixth house sextile progressed North Node and trine progressed South Node.
7. Progressed Mars in seventh house oppose progressed Saturn in first house.

VI. *Aspects from Jupiter*

1. Radical Jupiter in eleventh house sextile radical Saturn in first house.
2. Radical Jupiter in eleventh house square radical Uranus in second house.
3. Radical Jupiter in eleventh house square radical North Node and radical South Node.
4. Radical Jupiter in eleventh house square progressed Uranus in second house.

5. Radical Jupiter in eleventh house square progressed North Node and progressed South Node.
6. Progressed Jupiter in eleventh house square progressed North Node and progressed South Node.

VII. *Aspects from Uranus*

1. Radical Uranus in second house trine radical Neptune in sixth house.
2. Radical Uranus in second house oppose radical North Node and conjunct radical South Node.
3. Radical Uranus in second house trine progressed Neptune in sixth house.
4. Radical Uranus in second house oppose progressed North Node and conjunct progressed South Node.
5. Progressed Uranus in second house trine progressed Neptune in sixth house.
6. Progressed Uranus in second house oppose progressed North Node and conjunct progressed South Node.

VIII. *Aspects from Neptune*

1. Radical Neptune in sixth house sextile radical North Node and trine radical South Node.
2. Radical Neptune in sixth house sextile progressed North Node and trine progressed South Node.
3. Progressed Neptune in sixth house sextile progressed North Node and trine progressed South Node.

9

THE ASTROLOGICAL ANATOMY OF ASSASSINATIONS

We are already three-quarters of the way through the twentieth century, and it is startling to think that this century may go down in history as having the most assassinations. Although assassinations and other murders have the same end product of sudden death, there is more of an impact on people when they hear of an assassination, probably because within assassinations there are almost always the seeds of a Neptunian-inspired conspiracy, followed by a great deal of careful planning.

From time to time assassinations initiated by crime syndicates make the headlines, but sadly enough, we are practically immune to feeling sorrow and shock when these occur. However, when a head of state or some nationally beloved figure dies, then nations mourn and governments fret and worry, and the law-and-order authorities develop a frantic desire to produce a suspect, even if he sometimes appears to be only a scapegoat.

Few assassinations ever take place for the official reasons given out. Beyond the official reasons there are generally a mass of intrigue, a conspiring of minds, and a drastic need to remove someone who may interfere with another person's ambitions. There are times when even a murderer evokes compassion from the public; however, an assassin always arouses antagonistic feelings among the populace, many of whom would just as soon murder him themselves as leave him for the law to deal with. Assassinations take place because of inflamed passions and recreate the same passions in others. In doing research on the number of assassinations known to have taken place in the twentieth century, I am appalled that the number runs into several hundred—and that figure takes into account only the most famous ones. Who knows how many missing persons may have been assassinated, or what the true number of syndicate assassinations amounts to! Furthermore, attempted assassinations that were aborted could pull the statistics up to several thousand.

Consistent planetary patterns for assassination have not been established, probably because the plans for an assassination very often take place a long time before the deed is done. The astrologer cannot go by the Sun signs alone, since people of all Sun signs have met their death by assassination, and the strange thing is that some of the so-called benefic planets appear to be always in dramatic aspect when an assassination takes place. The Moon, Jupiter, and Venus are mainly responsible, and so I must conclude that the ultimate negatives of these signs must suddenly burgeon forth. The Moon influences the twists of fate which bring the assassinated and the assassin into each other's orbit. Jupiter is generally related to the position of power that the victim holds, and Venus is linked to the horrors that assassination cause. In addition, Pluto and Neptune join Mars in the conspiracy, providing the motivation and the action, to perform the deed; and the relationship of Mars, Venus, and Mercury affects the aftermath of an assassination—the reportage in the newspapers and the varied feelings of the people who become aware of it.

What would be fascinating for an astrologer to study would be the horoscope of the assassins—and I mean the *real* perpetrators of the crime, who are not necessarily the persons brought into the orbit of the law courts. Then we might get a more concise astrological picture of the truth behind assassinations, rather than the official version, which is rarely valid but is sufficient to give the Neptunian illusion that a person who does wrong is made to pay for the crime. The fate of the assassinated is sorrowful enough, but the fate of the assassin is a matter of conjecture if he is not apprehended and time is perhaps the greatest asset of all in covering up a conspiracy.

(Even as I write this on July 1, 1973, the news has come through that the Israeli Air Attaché to Washington has been assassinated in the state capital. This follows an eclipse of the Sun on June 30, affecting African borders and the Moslem Sheikdoms of the Persian Gulf.)

When the Archduke Francis Ferdinand and his wife of Austria-Hungary were assassinated on June 28, 1914, the event sparked off World War I. Uranus was transiting in Aquarius, Pluto in Cancer, and Neptune in Leo. Uranus, the planet of change, was giving the first big alert to the changing moods of people signified by Aquarius, the sign associated with the masses. Neptune, the planet of illusions and deceit, was in the royal sign of Leo. Each planet caused afflictions in the personal charts of the Archduke and his wife. On July 20, 1923, the famous bandit-president of Mexico, Pancho Villa, was assassinated, and at that time the Moon in Libra was in an unfavorable square aspect to the Sun in Cancer; Neptune was in Leo in conjunction with Mars, and Jupiter was just poised to enter Scorpio.

Each country of the world has known its own special sorrows through assassination. On August 20, 1940, Leon Trotsky was assassinated in Mexico. His assailant used a unique weapon—an icepick—to slaughter his Russian victim. At the time of the assassination, Mars had just entered Virgo and was opposed by the Moon in Pisces; Neptune, the planet of treachery, was in Virgo. Eight years later, on January 30, 1948, the world was shocked by the assassination of the great Indian leader Mahatma Gandhi. He was a man who had spent his life pleading for peace and nonviolent resistance, and yet he was doomed to die by the worst type of violence. At the time, Mars, providing the energy, was in Virgo, the sign associated with meticulous planning abilities. Mars was unfavorably aspected by Jupiter in Sagittarius, Jupiter symbolizing authority and Sagittarius philosophical thinking, which is often fallacious when it is adversely affected by the robust energies of Mars.

Ireland was always a fertile ground for political assassinations, and no less so today. Patrice Lumumba was assassinated in Africa, King Faisal II of Iraq and some of his family met the same fate, and there were numerous attempts to assassinate President Charles de Gaulle of France.

The United States had its greatest periods of national mourning when three assassinations took place within the space of a few years. President John F. Kennedy was the second Chief Executive to be assassinated in the twentieth century, Martin Luther King was raised to the status of a martyr after his assassination, and the assassination of Senator Robert Kennedy proved that lightning can, indeed, strike twice in the same family. Every one of these assassinations was as shocking to the nation as the famous assassination of President Abraham Lincoln a century ago.

Sudden death always brings shock with it, but the assassination of two members of the same family, both internationally known, has still left many people in a state of alternating horror and a wonder of how it could have happened. Every magazine has carried stories of the incredible series of calamities which befell the Kennedy family. Logic produces no satisfactory explanations. The world prides itself on logic, and at the same time is contemptuous of the occult sciences which extend beyond the realms of logic. If logic is the only answer, then it seems strange that young men should die before the promising flower of their youth can mature, while old men still live. The occultist and the astrologer accept another reason for this; they know that the Laws of Karma, of cause and effect, apply to the unbelieving as much as the believing.

Magazines are free to publish every detail about an assassination, yet if the person with psychic ability refers to it, then he or she is "in bad taste." I have had this accusation flung at me for no better reason than the fact that on a radio show in April 1968 in Philadelphia, I accurately predicted that an assassination of a national political figure would take place in June.

I have done the horoscopes of so many famous people that years ago when I charted the horoscope of Robert Kennedy, I was not impressed by his name—but I *was* impressed and horrified by what I found in the horoscope. The fact that I was within the vicinity of the Ambassador Hotel in Los Angeles when the assassination took place produced no horror in me at all, for I had experienced it when I did the horoscope, and I had already grown to accept it.

On going through my files recently, I was impressed by the horoscopic likeness in the natal charts of the two murdered Kennedy brothers, almost appalling in their similarity. Both had the Sun in the lethal eighth house. John Kennedy had Mars, the lesser malefic planet, exactly on the cusp of the eighth, in its most powerful position. Robert had Saturn, the greater malefic planet, in the identical position—equally as powerful, equally as lethal. He also had Mars, Saturn, and the Sun in Scorpio. Astrologically speaking, the real villain of the horoscope was the treacherous planet of Neptune which closely afflicted the Sun in the natal eighth house at twenty-four and a half degrees Leo to twenty-seven and a half degrees Scorpio. The setting is correct for what the ancient astrologers called the "Mark of Doom," which signified that at the height of popularity and acclaim by the crowd, the same crowd would strike back and bring destruction. How right those old astrologers were! Robert Kennedy reached the climax of popularity in the California campaign and met his death with cheers ringing in his ears.

Other detriments were found in his horoscope. Saturn, the great teaching planet, which is also the restrictor, was in eighteen degrees of Scorpio and by transit adversely squared its own natal place and conjoined the Sun. Pluto, the planet associated with unexpected, often deadly happenings, was also in the southwest angle of Robert Kennedy's natal chart, as it was in his brother's. It is significant that Los Angeles, the place where the Senator met death by an assassin's bullet, is southwest of Massachusetts, where he was born.

Already the Kennedy family has had six distinct tragedies which became known to the public *after* the event. The person with psychic ability does not believe that as a man sows, so shall he reap—unless the theory is applied to the credits and debits of past incarnations. Logically, the Kennedys are a well-meaning, decent-living family, renowned for their firm adherence to the Roman Catholic faith. If the idea of reaping what is sown applies to only one incarnation, then logic would say that every Kennedy should die in bed at a ripe old age, after a full, meaningful life. Nothing in their present lives could possibly be construed as reaping the kind of malignant harvest that has come to all of them. Even Senator Edward Kennedy has endured terrible accidents, plus the scandal of Chappaquiddick. Joseph Kennedy, despite his fantastic success in business, was for years an incapacitated human being, and it needs little imagination to realize the sorrow which the tragedies in the family brought to the elder Kennedy and his wife. So the question is posed: *why* all this in one family?

The Laws of Karma, associated with cause and effect and the survival of the spirit after death, give rise to the belief that many people are linked together by such laws prevailing through many incarnations. Most of us have evolved through numerous experiences to come to this present life. From the occult point of view, it seems unlikely that the Kennedys achieved their present position of eminence and tragedy merely by what they have done in this life. It is not a case of an all-vengeful God exacting retribution, but simply that in past incarnations the Kennedys had their moments of benevolence, and also their cruelties. This explanation will not be acceptable to many who follow orthodox religions, but to the occultist and astrologer, the Laws of Karma make sense in a chaotic world in which assassinations take place.

Those who think that the Kennedy family is just "unfortunate" in the violence and calamity which have walked hand in hand with almost unprecedented affluence and recognition, have yet to prove that there is a logical cause. Every question has its answer, just as every problem always has a solution and every disease a remedy. If logic does not provide the answer, then the curious person must expand his thinking and consider another force which plays a vital part in man's life, maturity, and death. The laws of the universe are also the basic laws of man's nature and life. The liaison between cause and effect, which the occultist and astrologer call Karma, go on relentlessly. "Karma" is a word that we should begin to understand a little better in the future. Slowly, the astrologer, the occultist, and the prophets throughout the world, extend the horizons of the mind so that words, philosophies, and ways of life that are different may not be condemned by lack of understanding.

The aftereffects of an assassination of a nationally prominent person last long after the first shock and horror die away. Men begin to live with suspicions, the national scene becomes overrun with Neptunian-inspired rumors, and everyone has a theory about what really happened. People in high position need not be envied, since they go into office knowing that there are risks to the job. In Great Britain every head that has ever worn a royal crown has known some uneasy moments, and it is always lonely to be in the top position in the government of the United States. President William Taft, born with his Sun in Virgo, said, "This is the lonesomest place in the world." And President Thomas Jefferson, born with his Sun in Aries, on relinquishing his office, remarked, "Never did a prisoner released from his chains, feel such a sense of relief as I shall on shaking off the shackles of power."

Such sentiments may well be in the secret thoughts of President Richard M. Nixon, born with his Sun in Capricorn and harassed by his ruling planet, Saturn, the taskmaster of the zodiac—the relentless cutter-down of people in high places.

On Christmas Eve of 1973 a total eclipse of the Sun in Capricorn took place, posing a threat by enemies to chiefs of state. Such a solar eclipse is never favorable to the United States, a Sun-in-Cancer nation. The last days of 1973 indeed provoked another period of national horror for this country, with conspiracies again hitting the headlines—while truth remains locked in a well of turgid waters.

10

THE EXPLOSIVE EARTH

And, behold, the veil of the temple was rent in twain from the top to the bottom; and the earth did quake, and the rocks rent.
Matthew XXVII, 51

When we learn that an earthquake has hit a specific area of the world, we are inclined to think it is an isolated event which may not happen again for many years. The truth is that the 1,200-odd seismograph stations throughout the world officially record about 500,000 tremors each year. One-fifth of these can be heard or felt, and over one thousand cause real damage to life and property.

Some places are more vulnerable than others, and the United States always seems to look toward California as the principal area where a massive quake is likely to hit. There is a good reason for this, for the sinister San Andreas fault runs for 650 miles through the state, boring below the surface of downtown San Francisco and skirting Los Angeles. Further inland and parallel with the San Andreas fault are the stretches of the Hayward fault, running through Oakland and the East Bay, and the Calaveras fault slightly to the east. They are all part of a circum-Pacific seismic region that loops around the rim of the ocean from Chile to Alaska to New Zealand; in this area, something like 80 percent of the world's earthquakes occur. The predictions of Edgar Cayce have added to the uneasiness which many Americans feel about California. However, the fact is that only two states in this country—Texas and Florida—can be regarded as zero earthquake probability zones. It may be some consolation to know that if earthquakes occur in rapid succession over the main portion of the United States, Walt Disney World near Orlando, Florida, will be quite safe.

Earthquakes threaten the midwestern states as much as they do California, and a severe quake in a heavily populated midwest city such as Chicago, St. Louis, Cincinnati, or Memphis would be just as disastrous as one of similar magnitude in California. The hard bedrock, even if much further down from the surface of the earth in the midwest, nevertheless makes buildings there very vulnerable to shock waves. The Midwest has the doubtful distinction of being the scene in 1811 of one of the three fiercest earthquakes ever known in this country. Of course the damage was much less than it would be today, because at that time the Midwest was sparsely populated.

Millions of dollars are being spent today on earthquake research throughout the world, and every year astrologers check charts in an effort to discover if and when an earthquake will strike. The official research scientists admit that even when they are aware of an approaching earthquake, there is little that can be done to evacuate large masses of people in time—and astrologers are in the same position. In places such as Los Angeles and San Francisco, plans have been developed for dealing with emergencies *after* they have happened but it is depressing to know that one of the main rescue centers and the communications area is actually built on a critical area of the San Andreas fault!

The planetary configurations for earthquakes have many characteristics not found in the patterns of other natural disasters. It was not out of superstitious belief that ancient astrologers were afraid of eclipses. The studying of eclipses gives the first clues according to which house the two luminaries are making the eclipse in. In ascertaining all vital information concerning natural disasters and inclement weather, it is important for the astrologer today to know where and when eclipses will occur each year. All earthquakes occur when the Sun and Moon are in close aspect to each other. This characteristic is so basic that some earthquakes occur *exactly* at the time of a full moon. Most natural disasters take their cue from the *solar* eclipse, but earthquakes do a switch on this: It is the *lunar* eclipse that precedes an earthquake. At the time of the lunar eclipse, all the forces of energy in the heavy planets are at the gathering stage. There is always a major aspect to the fourth house at the same time that the ascendant is involved in massive contacts.

In 1924 an astrologer-historian, Mr. W. G. Old, said, "The mythology of Neptune seems to support the notion that it has much to do with earthquakes." It is a fact that some of the more recent earthquakes have happened immediately after the conjunctions or oppositions of Uranus, Mars and Neptune.

Most contemporary astrologers agree with the ancient astronomers who stated that "When an eclipse of the Sun or Moon takes place in conjunction with Mercury, it will generate in the atmosphere turbulent, sharp, and variable winds, together with thunder and lightning, accompanied by sudden chasms in the earth and earthquakes."

Sir Isaac Newton was inclined to believe that a new or full moon "with certain planets in the first degree of Taurus and especially the Pleiades, will produce earthquakes."

In 1953 Dr. R. Tomaschek checked the placement of all the planets at the time of 134 earthquakes, and found that Uranus was always close to the midheaven at the time and place of a disaster. In most cases Neptune and Pluto, the two slowest-moving planets, were aligned across the solar system. Mars provides the catalystic energy to set off an earthquake, and Uranus provides the influence of its ability to create the unexpected; Neptune influences the weather before a quake.

At the time the 1906 earthquake struck San Francisco, Uranus was only within six minutes of arc from the midheaven and Neptune was directly on the nadir, in exact opposition to Uranus. In 1923, when an earthquake struck Tokyo and Yokohama, Uranus was sixteen minutes of arc past the meridian of Tokyo. In the Assam, India, earthquake of 1950, Uranus was within twenty-five minutes of arc from the midheaven. At the time of the Alaskan earthquake in 1964, Uranus was within a few degrees of the midheaven and the full Moon was exactly conjunct with Mars, backed up with strong aspects from Venus, Uranus, Neptune, and Pluto.

Conjunctions of Jupiter and Mars influence earthquakes by expansion, but Saturn operates by contraction. The linking up of conjunctions or an eclipse causes lengthy trigger points of energy throughout the solar system. It is rather like the bumping that occurs when trains are shunting coaches: The engine bumps the first coach, the first coach bumps the second, all through the line each bump adding a little more energy until at the end of the line there is a tremendously powerful force.

Earthquakes are likely to happen when there is planetary stress in evidence across the 90 degree to 270 degree sections of a chart—that is, from the nadir (90 degrees) to the midheaven (270 degrees)—and when Jupiter, Saturn, and Neptune form a T-square from 90 to 270 degrees.

Alexis Perrey of France compared the solar-lunar positions of about 24,000 earthquakes and came to the conclusion that earthquakes are most drastic soon after the Sun and Moon are in line with the earth, and when the Moon is in perigee, that is, at that point of the Moon's orbit which is nearest to earth. Apogee, of course, is that point when the Moon's orbit is farthest away from the earth. Dr. C. G. Knott, another seismic researcher, agreed with Perrey and he used thousands of Japanese earthquakes as his controls. He added to Perrey's conclusions his own findings that the tendency to earthquakes increased at times when the Moon was directly overhead at the location of the disturbances. A classical example of this theory occurred on July 26, 1963, when four-fifths of the city of Skopje in Yugoslavia was destroyed. The Moon was directly overhead the meridian of Skopje in nineteen degrees of Libra.

In all known cases of earthquakes, Mars, Uranus, and Jupiter are always at critical points in the heavens, cooperating fully with the dark forces of Pluto, which is generally lined up with Venus.

In May 1973 I wrote down a few ideas about the forthcoming eclipses of the year and, following my usual practice, had the document notarized. (I recommend that anyone making predictions, whether astrological or psychic, do this. A notarized document is a record which is readily accepted by everyone, and it can be valid proof that you are not predicting after the event, since it is always dated.) In my May research on eclipses the following was written down and notarized (on May 21, 1973):

Mars reaches a point just square to the solar eclipse of June 30th at 8.5 degrees in Cancer on July 3rd and 4th. Since this is the only major planetary influence to that point during the entire succeeding year, there is a strong possibility of an earthquake, probably along the line of the southern limit of the eclipse, slightly toward the eastern end where it crosses southwest and south Africa. It appears to be a malefic eclipse because it takes place right in the south node of the Moon, quincunx Neptune and Jupiter and within orb of a conjunction to Saturn.

The lunar eclipse of July 15th has a very malefic cosmic cross involving Uranus in opposition to Mars, both planets square to the Sun and Moon opposition at 22 degrees and 51 minutes of Cancer. A chart set up for the lunar eclipse in the area of the United States covered by Mountain Standard Time would put the malefic planets in opposition across the meridian. The great Rocky Mountains could get a good shaking up during the middle of July. Add to the other aspects the heliocentric ones of Saturn squaring Venus and the earth squaring Uranus on the 14th and 15th, and we find ourselves likely to get a double dose of malice in this lunar eclipse.

(Incidentally, there should be a big drop in the stock market between July 7–15, as well as some serious and earth-shaking events concerning the President.)

> The Sun squaring Uranus in geocentric perspective adds to the difficulties. More turbulence on July 18th and 19th, with heliocentric aspects in effect. Mercury squaring Jupiter, Mercury conjunct earth and Venus conjunct Pluto. This is followed by a geocentric aspect of Mars in opposition to Uranus, indicating that travel problems and communications will be upset, especially during the period from July 12th–23rd.
>
> In the last few days of July, Jupiter and the earth line up in conjunction in heliocentric aspect, together with Mercury conjunct Mars, Mercury square Neptune, and Venus conjunct Uranus. More storms, land disturbances, and a series of tornadoes with the southwest U.S.A. bearing the brunt of it. A month to be remembered.

On Monday, July 2, 1973, a call from Mr. Neil Murray of Los Angeles informed me that a larger than usual tremor had been felt in his city, and he also felt that something troublesome would be felt in Los Angeles about the middle of July. Of course there have been numerous cries about earthquakes in the Los Angeles area, so much so that anyone now making a prediction is apt to be reminded about the times when the earthquakes did *not* appear.

It is nothing new to predict earthquakes and other natural disasters astrologically or psychically. Sir Isaac Newton accurately predicted tremendous and unusual atmospheric conditions for England beginning in February 1750. He based his predictions on the fact that Jupiter would be near enough to earth on the date of an eclipse while the Moon would also be at its closest point to earth. (Incidentally, Newton never knew that his prediction came true, for it occurred many years after his death.)

In ancient times a scientist called Anaximander erected the first observatory in Lacedaemon in Greece. From there he accurately predicted that the city would be subjected to an earthquake. (He did not predict that the city would be destroyed at the time of the quake, however; otherwise he may have had second thoughts about erecting the observatory there.) The Greek philosopher Democritus, also had great success in predicting earthquakes and was astute enough to suggest that other planets would in time be found beyond Saturn.

Of course the scientific investigation of seismic changes has now taken precedence over the astrological predictions of modern-day astrologers. Few have the time to make the lengthy calculations necessary, and all astrological research on natural disasters has to be financed by private means and a lot of dedication on the part of the astrologer. The government spends several million dollars a year on investigating earthquakes—and its group of experts does not include even one astrologer!

The Age of Aquarius, though, is upon us—and in this period we can expect astrology to cease being the

Cinderella of the sciences. Six astrologers doing nothing else but analyzing the eclipses each year would cost the taxpayers much less than any other type of research.

Among the worst earthquake disasters of modern times are the following:

November 1, 1775 More than 80,000 persons were killed in an earthquake felt over an area of one million square miles in Portugal. Thousands of persons were swallowed up by the ocean. At this time Pluto was transiting in the earth sign of Capricorn.

February 5–March 27, 1783 A series of earthquakes on and around Calabria in Italy destroyed 181 towns and caused 30,000 casualties. Pluto was in the air sign of Aquarius.

February 4, 1797 Forty-one thousand lives were lost in a series of earthquakes around the city of Quito in Ecuador. Pluto was transiting in Aquarius.

December 16, 1811 One of the most destructive earthquakes ever known in North America took place in southeastern Missouri. It ruined 50,000 square miles of farmland, and the violent earth shakes were felt in Arkansas, Kentucky, and Tennessee. At this time Pluto was transiting in Pisces.

November 19, 1822 An upheaval of land caused the ocean to recede and took thousands of lives by drowning. This happened in Valparaiso, Chile, and Pluto was transiting in Pisces.

1835 The entire city of Concepción in Chile was destroyed by an earthquake when Pluto was transiting in Aries.

October 28, 1891 In the Mino and Owari provinces of Japan 230,000 homes were destroyed, with the loss of life of 7,200. At this time Pluto was transiting in Gemini.

1896 A submarine quake at Sanriku in Japan resulted in the death of 28,000 people. Less unusual earthquakes occurred in the same year at Kamaiski and Robugo. Pluto was transiting in Gemini.

April 18, 1906 The most disastrous earth tremor in the history of the United States, estimated at 8.5 on the Richter Scale, devastated San Francisco. The quake was followed by a fire in which 452 people were killed and 28,188 buildings were destroyed. Pluto was transiting in Gemini.

December 28, 1908 The cities of Messina and Baratti in Italy were flattened in an earthquake which took a toll of 80,000 lives. Pluto was transiting in Gemini.

January 13, 1915 Thirty thousand people were killed around Avezzano in central Italy. Pluto was just making its transition from Gemini to Cancer.

September 1, 1923 The greatest of all twentieth-century disasters occurred in Tokyo and Yokohama in Japan. The casualty toll was 99,331 dead, 576,262 homes destroyed, and millions left homeless. The fire damage alone was about $5 million. Pluto was transiting in Cancer.

March 10, 1933 An earthquake measuring 6.3 on the Richter Scale struck Long Beach, California, leaving 120 people dead, several thousands injured, and property losses amounting to $40 million. It was the second most severe earthquake in the United States, and Pluto was transiting in Cancer.

May 21–May 29, 1960 A series of violent earthquakes with Richter magnitude up to 9.0 took place in Chile. The death toll was 5,700 lives, and millions were left homeless. Pluto was transiting in Virgo.

September 1, 1962 More than 10,000 died in northern Iran. Pluto was transiting in Virgo.

July 26, 1963 Four-fifths of the city of Skopje, Yugoslavia, was destroyed, 1,011 people lost their lives, and the injured numbered 3,350. Pluto was transiting in Virgo.

March 27, 1964 A fierce earthquake occurred in Alaska, bringing death to 114 people and causing $700 million damage. Pluto was transiting in Virgo.

August 19–August 23, 1966 A series of quakes killed 2,529 people in eastern Turkey and left 100,000 homeless. Pluto was transiting in Virgo.

July 29, 1967 Two severe earthquakes of Richter magnitude of 7.8 and 6.8 destroyed one hundred towns in northeastern Iran. About 22,000 people died and 100,000 were left homeless. Pluto was in Virgo.

September 1969 Two earthquakes shook southern Mexico in an area already reeling from disastrous floods. The first registered 5.0 and the second 5.3 on the Richter Scale. There was little loss of life, but considerable damage to property amounting to about $50 million.

October 2, 1969 Two earthquakes measuring 5.6 and 5.5 on the Richter Scale hit the Santa Rosa area of California and were preceded by minor tremors on October 1. Pluto was transiting in Virgo.

April 7, 1970 An earthquake occurred in the Philippines with a magnitude of 7.3, killing 200 people and causing considerable damage to property. At this time Pluto was transiting in Virgo.

May 31, 1970 An earthquake ravaged the Peruvian Andes, wiping out scores of villages, bringing death to 50,000 and causing hundreds of millions of dollars worth of damage.

February 9, 1971 An earthquake shook the San Fernando and San Gabriel valleys in California. The Richter measurement was 6.5, eight people died, and there was damage amounting to several million dollars. Pluto was transiting in Virgo.

December 15, 1971 An earthquake measuring 7.8 on the Richter Scale was recorded off the east coast of Siberias Kamchatka Peninsula. Pluto was transiting in Libra.

April 26, 1972 A major earthquake occurred in the Philippines registering 7.3 on the Richter Scale. Officially no loss of life was reported, but there was considerable loss of property. Pluto was transiting in Virgo.

11

THE ASTROLOGICAL EVOLUTION OF COUNTRIES

Astrologers are aware that every country and every city are under the influence of one of the twelve signs of the zodiac. However, many astrologers forget that just as the chart of an individual must be progressed to bring it up to date each year, so the zodiacal influences change in the progress of a city or country.

An ancient country or city may well go through many changes within its life span. England has always been considered an Arian country; it went through all the obvious characteristics of the Arian influences on exploration by pioneers. Then it moved on to a time when it was building a great empire solid enough to be associated with a typically Taurean period of growth and consolidation. England also had a period when great literary activity was at its peak, and this was its Geminian period. After World War II there was a frantic period of building houses and providing homes for masses of people, and this was its Cancerian period. Today the influences of Leo are present; England is still involved with its royalty, and has strong nationalistic feelings and a sense that the country is one large family with the Queen at the head. Leo's influences are just about ready to give way to a strong Virgo influence, with the advent of Britain into the Common Market and a concern with land and food, complete with more attention to diet and a clean environment.

Every country goes through this progression, not excluding the United States. At the time when its Constitution was formed in 1776, and for quite a long time after, America was a typically Cancerian country. It opened its arms to immigrants and became a home to thousands of displaced people. It was the Mother Country of all unfortunates, where they could be nurtured, be loved, and get a feeling of belonging—all typically Cancerian attributes.

But times change through progress, and the United States proceeded to take on Leo characteristics: an imperialism emphasized by military prowess abroad, an inability to take criticism, and at its helm a typically Leonine father-figure image in the form of the President. Like any Leo father chastising his children, Mr. Nixon assured the American people that everything he does is for their own good. Economic phases One, Two, and Three have all been for the good of his American "children" from the President's point of view. High taxes are good for them and the war against

Vietnam was for their own good. Most of all, the inflation from which the country suffers is typical of a Leo zodiacal regime, and affluence is flaunted by people in high places, including the President. His normal Capricorn instincts would never have allowed him to own a property in California and another in Key Biscayne, but the arrogance of the Leo influences makes it much easier for him to do this.

However, the United States is just moving into its Virgo phase, when self-analysis is going to dominate; there will be some cruel moments of self-criticism, which we began to get a glimpse of during the Senate hearings of the Watergate affair. With the self-criticism will come a period of national guilt. But the more positive aspects of the Virgo cycle will be a greater interest in underprivileged people and a really sincere attempt to clean up the environment. We shall make a big effort also to get back to a more wholesome diet, with fewer chemicals and synthetic foods. The Mercurial mind of Virgo will continue to produce some great feats in technology, electronics, and more computerized programs. Education likely will be designed to make students less competitive and more geared to teamwork.

Japan started its life as a Scorpio country, very secretive and mysterious about its internal affairs. But with the need for foreign trading, it is under the influence of Sagittarius. In fact, it will thrive and survive only because of its ability to mingle with foreigners, to buy land in other countries, and to set up commercial pacts abroad. It will remain under the influence of Sagittarius until A.D. 2000, but once it has completely exploited all its efforts to gain recognition throughout the world through business instead of war, it will become Capricornian, able to control some of the major markets of the world with law and order. What it gains now in business territories, Japan will hold possessively and never relinquish.

China presents an interesting zodiacal progression through the signs. It was once a typically Libran country, with the usual Libran appreciation of love and beauty, constantly creating items of unbelievable artistry. Yet behind the beauty was the Libran secondary characteristic of aggression, and this began to dominate the creativity. So the Libran involvement with social and legal controls came about. The zodiacal scales began to rock violently; constant wars and social upheavals were in evidence. Then the country went into its Scorpio trend, secret and mysterious, cut off for years from the rest of the world but always aware of what was happening in other countries. Scorpio is associated with death and regeneration, and both came when Mao Tse-tung took office. Through many deaths and Scorpion malefic acts, he gradually brought about the regeneration of the whole country, to balance the old Libran artistic creativity with the new life in which manual work is regarded as equal to that done by an intellectual. It is interesting to remember that one of the oldest symbols of the world is the Chinese Yin-Yang, whose complementary halves manage to achieve a perfect balance. China has done that in the last few years; even though we may be critical of how the balance was achieved, we have to admit that today China still produces its art while the working peasant has gained a status he could never have had during the fully artistic Libran period.

Today China is moving out of its Scorpio cycle to make the first moves into Sagittarius, the sign associated with foreigners. No longer are foreigners thought of as "white-faced devils," because, like Japan, China needs some of the benefits from other countries. Her sense of timing was excellent; the first moves came after President Nixon became the first high government official in twenty-five years to enter China. Too, China may have learned a lesson from aggression and now seems to understand that there is no need to go to war when the hand of friendship can be grasped and then filled with bounties from another country.

Russia was once the most typically Leonine country of all, with rulers absolute and ultimate in authority. Then she moved for a very brief time into Virgo through the influence of her famous Catherine the Great. From this she moved rapidly into Libra, complete with its artistic and architectural glories, but always with the Libran aggressiveness. At the time of the murder of the Romanov family and the taking over of the country by the Bolsheviks, Russia was under the influences of Scorpio. Then she passed rapidly from the secrecy which the bloodshed necessitated to realize that she must be in contact with other countries, and the Sagittarius influences took over. Today, Russia is Capricornian, conserving her own energies, possessive of her land, with fine engineers and technicians as her heroes. In the next twenty-five years she will move into Aquarius, and in less than a hundred years will achieve the brotherhood of man which was the academic principle behind the bloody revolution of 1917. She will also express something of a little-discussed trait of the Age of Aquarius—the move by many countries to form a police state in which the Capricornian love of law and order will be carried on with very effective results. It will crystallize and restrict all individual initiative, allowing little room for the expansion of the individual, and everyone will be performing regular duties as team members for the good of the whole.

For as long as I can remember, the black race has been astrologically classified as Pisces, feeling all the restrictive influences of this sign. Also the black race has been as diffuse as the ruling planet Neptune, its members scattering their energies but also influencing the world with typically Piscean characteristics of dancing and music. Around the early 1950's they moved from Pisces to Aries, and they began to use some of the Arian's ability to pioneer, to press forward for what they considered good for them—albeit the pressure was sometimes applied headstrongly. This happened in Africa, and it is happening in the United States. Every black man who forced his way out of his ghetto was showing an Arian pioneering spirit. As a race, the black people have not yet moved into Taurus, when they will gain more of the material resources of the world, but they are rapidly moving into this phase by forming themselves into groups for cooperative buying of food, houses, and other commodities. They should enter their Taurean period by the early 1980's, first by infiltrating into such typically Taurean areas as being food merchants, then as landlords and landowners. Finally, by about the year 2000, they will enter the Geminian stage of their progressive lifestyle and move into the realms and influences of the sign associated with communication, literary efforts, and extravagant affluency. After that, the black race will consolidate, own more homes, and finally move into the influences of the royal sign of Leo about the turn of the century. The black man will have his own empires to rule over with the same arrogance and pride that all Leos feel when they have attained what they know to be their rightful place in the Sun.

As we move toward the year 2000, we shall be well into the Age of Aquarius and there will have been a great shift in the balance of power of nations. We should not expect the white race to remain supreme rulers of the earth. Interracial marriages will be more in evidence, and there will be a lessening of the number of religions in the world. The passage of Neptune through Sagittarius, the sign associated with religious and philosophical thinking, will see a reduction of power by the Church of Rome, with probably only one more Pope yet to be elected. The Church of England will again be much more interested in healing than any other church has ever been and will rival the great historic monasteries which originally provided medical help for the community. The strength and power of the Church of Rome will be replaced by the Mormon Church, whose steady infiltration into every known part of the world has been quietly and effectively performed since the beginning of the century and has escalated in recent years. It will fit in very well with the Age of Aquarius, since it has already established itself as a church of group activities designed to make people of all races feel the bond of Aquarian Age brotherhood. Most of the other churches will fall by the wayside and will be in the same position that Wicca was in when it was forced to go underground and become a secret society.

Since the Age of Aquarius is associated with brotherhood (in the masculine sense), its seems contradictory to state that a new factor will arise in religion, with women taking high office. But from Japan we shall see the rise of an enormous matriarchal church, very much inspired by a combination of all the known nature religions, and with a woman at its head.

Uranus, the ruler of the Age of Aquarius, is the planet associated with inventions, and as we approach the year 2000, life as we live it today will seem as primitive as the life described to us by our own grandparents. The children of today will live to see much smaller housing units, because of the shortage of land for the increased population. But they will know every possible push-button aid to living. Brownouts due to electrical power shortages will seem as remote as the oil lamps at the turn of the century, as nuclear energy at last begins to be used to better advantage. Canned music will still be popular, but to fit the smaller houses, everything will be miniaturized. We can expect to have playable discs smaller than a silver dollar, as well as books on microfilm. The push of a button on a telephone will bring us the image of the person we are talking to, and we will not be chained to the telephone cord and mouthpiece.

Family life in small units is likely to give way to communes where children are looked after during the parents' working hours. There will be every encouragement to give a home to children who are deprived of their parents. Love will be a much more abstract thing, rather than a personal one, and artificial insemination will be legally available for any woman who requests it, with or without the institution of marriage. It will not be unusual for a woman to have a child, raise him or her with the aid of the commune, and ignore the need for a father image. This is not to say that love and sex will be restricted for those who still prefer this way of life; it is simply that there will be many more options available—including the greater acceptance of homosexual relationships. Enormous strides will be made in the occult sciences, with university courses in telepathy, psychokinesis, the development of extrasensory perception and astral-projection, and astrology will be an honorable science.

It will be a great and glorious age, with men and

women still destined to be heroes and heroines and pioneers, and there will be little discrimination between the sexes when it comes to extending space travel activities.

The big hurdle to overcome before this Aquarian Shangri-la is 1984. It could be Armageddon, but the age-old Darwinian theory will prevail: There is still a place in the world for the survival of the fittest.

So mote it be.

12

APPENDIX

URANUS—Dates in the Various Zodiacal Signs

October 1800 to October 1807—Libra
November 1807 to December 1813—Scorpio
January 1814 to November 1820—Sagittarius
December 1820 to February 1828—Capricorn
March 1828 to February 1836—Aquarius
March 1836 to February 2, 1844—Pisces
February 3, 1844, to July 5, 1850—Aries
July 6, 1850, to September 4, 1850—Taurus
September 5, 1850, to April 14, 1851—Aries
April 15, 1851, to May 31, 1858—Taurus
June 1, 1858, to January 3, 1859—Gemini
January 4, 1859, to March 11, 1859—Taurus
March 12, 1859, to June 25, 1865—Gemini
June 26, 1865, to February 21, 1866—Cancer
February 22, 1866, to March 22, 1866—Gemini
March 23, 1866, to September 12, 1871—Cancer
September 13, 1871, to January 1, 1872—Leo
January 2, 1872, to June 27, 1872—Cancer

June 28, 1872, to August 24, 1878—Leo
August 25, 1878, to October 13, 1884—Virgo
October 14, 1884, to April 11, 1885—Libra
April 12, 1885, to July 28, 1885—Virgo
July 29, 1885, to December 9, 1890—Libra
December 10, 1890, to April 4, 1891—Scorpio
April 5, 1891, to September 25, 1891—Libra
September 26, 1891, to December 1, 1897—Scorpio
December 2, 1897, to July 3, 1898—Sagittarius
July 4, 1898, to September 10, 1898—Scorpio
September 11, 1898, to December 19, 1904—Sagittarius
December 20, 1904, to January 30, 1912—Capricorn
January 31, 1912, to September 4, 1912—Aquarius
September 5, 1912, to November 11, 1912—Capricorn
November 12, 1912, to March 31, 1919—Aquarius
April 1, 1919, to August 16, 1919—Pisces
August 17, 1919, to January 21, 1920—Aquarius
January 22, 1920, to March 30, 1927—Pisces
March 31, 1927, to November 4, 1927—Aries
November 5, 1927, to January 12, 1928—Pisces
January 13, 1928, to June 6, 1934—Aries
June 7, 1934, to October 10, 1934—Taurus
October 11, 1934, to March 27, 1935—Aries
March 28, 1935, to August 7, 1941—Taurus
August 8, 1941, to October 5, 1941—Gemini
October 6, 1941, to May 14, 1942—Taurus
May 15, 1942, to August 30, 1948—Gemini
August 31, 1948, to November 12, 1948—Cancer
November 13, 1948, to June 10, 1949—Gemini
June 11, 1949, to August 24, 1955—Cancer
August 25, 1955, to January 28, 1956—Leo
January 29, 1956, to June 9, 1956—Cancer
June 10, 1956, to November 1, 1961—Leo
November 2, 1961, to January 10, 1962—Virgo

January 11, 1962, to August 9, 1962—Leo
August 10, 1962, to September 28, 1968—Virgo
September 29, 1968, to May 21, 1969—Libra
May 22, 1969, to June 24, 1969—Virgo
June 25, 1969, to December 14, 1974—Libra

NEPTUNE—Dates in the Various Zodiacal Signs

December 1806 to January 1820—Sagittarius
February 1820 to June 1820—Capricorn
July 1820 to November 1820—Sagittarius
December 1820 to January 1834—Capricorn
February 1834 to August 1834—Aquarius
September 1834 to November 1834—Capricorn
December 1834 to April 1847—Aquarius
May 1847 to August 1847—Pisces
September 1847 to January 1848—Aquarius
February 1848 to April 13, 1861—Pisces
April 14, 1861, to October 1, 1861—Aries
October 2, 1861, to February 13, 1862—Pisces
February 14, 1862, to June 6, 1874—Aries
June 7, 1874, to September 30, 1874—Taurus
October 1, 1874, to April 6, 1875—Aries
April 7, 1875, to August 15, 1887—Taurus
August 16, 1887, to September 21, 1887—Gemini
September 22, 1887, to May 25, 1888—Taurus
May 26, 1888, to December 27, 1888—Gemini
December 28, 1888, to March 20, 1889—Taurus
March 21, 1889, to July 19, 1901—Gemini
July 20, 1901, to December 25, 1901—Cancer
December 26, 1901, to May 20, 1902—Gemini
May 21, 1902, to September 22, 1914—Cancer
September 23, 1914, to December 14, 1914—Leo

December 15, 1914, to July 18, 1915—Cancer
July 19, 1915, to March 19, 1916—Leo
March 20, 1916, to May 1, 1916—Cancer
May 2, 1916, to September 20, 1928—Leo
September 21, 1928, to February 19, 1929—Virgo
February 20, 1929, to July 23, 1929—Leo
July 24, 1929, to October 3, 1942—Virgo
October 4, 1942, to April 18, 1943—Libra
April 19, 1943, to August 2, 1943—Virgo
August 3, 1943, to December 23, 1955—Libra
December 24, 1955, to March 11, 1956—Scorpio
March 12, 1956, to October 18, 1956—Libra
October 19, 1956, to June 16, 1957—Scorpio
June 17, 1957, to August 4, 1957—Libra
August 5, 1957, to January 4, 1970—Scorpio
January 5, 1970, to May 3, 1970—Sagittarius
May 4, 1970, to November 6, 1970—Scorpio
November 7, 1970, to February 3, 1984—Sagittarius

PLUTO—Dates in the Various Zodiacal Signs

1762 to 1777—Capricorn
1777 to September 1799—Aquarius
October 1799 to May 1821—Pisces
June 1821 to August 1821—Aries
September 1821 to March 1822—Pisces
April 1822 to October 1822—Aries
November 1822 to January 1823—Pisces
February 1823 to June 1850—Aries
July 1850 to September 1850—Taurus
October 1850 to May 26, 1851—Aries
May 27, 1851, to October 28, 1851—Taurus
October 29, 1851, to April 13, 1852—Aries
April 14, 1852, to December 2, 1852—Taurus
December 3, 1852, to February 16, 1853—Aries

February 17, 1853, to July 29, 1882—Taurus
July 30, 1882, to September 27, 1882—Gemini
September 28, 1882, to June 24, 1883—Taurus
June 25, 1883, to November 27, 1883—Gemini
November 28, 1883, to April 23, 1884—Taurus
April 24, 1884, to September 24, 1912—Gemini
September 25, 1912, to October 2, 1912—Cancer
October 3, 1912, to July 12, 1913—Gemini
July 13, 1913, to December 25, 1913—Cancer
December 26, 1913, to May 23, 1914—Gemini
May 24, 1914, to October 8, 1937—Cancer
October 9, 1937, to November 15, 1937—Leo
November 16, 1937, to August 5, 1938—Cancer
August 6, 1938, to February 7, 1939—Leo
February 8, 1939, to June 15, 1939—Cancer
June 16, 1939, to October 19, 1956—Leo
October 20, 1956, to January 16, 1957—Virgo
January 17, 1957, to August 18, 1957—Leo
August 19, 1957, to October 4, 1971—Virgo
October 5, 1971, to April 17, 1972—Libra
April 18, 1972, to July 30, 1972—Virgo
July 31, 1972, to November 20, 1983—Libra
November 21, 1983, to May 20, 1984—Scorpio
May 21, 1984, to July 29, 1984—Libra
July 30, 1984, to January 1, 1995—Scorpio
January 2, 1995, to April 22, 1995—Sagittarius
April 23, 1995, to November 18, 1995—Scorpio
November 19, 1995, to 2009—Sagittarius

KEY TO PLANETARY ASPECTS

Aspecting Planets	*Conjunction*	*Positive*	*Negative*	*Refers to*
Sun—Moon	Concentrated	Assured	Contradictory	Basic character
	Integrated	Confident	Irresolute	
	Self-sufficient	Fortunate	Paradoxical	
Sun—Mercury	Acute	Intelligent	Ambivalent	Practical mind
	Alert	Perspicacious	Undiscriminating	
	Attentive	Rational	Vacillating	
Sun—Venus	Elegant	Alluring	Luxury-loving	Personal magnetism
	Gracious	Attractive	Indulgent	
	Loving	Charming	Insincere	
Sun—Mars	Demonstrative	Candid	Aggressive	Vital force
	Pioneering	Courageous	Inflammatory	
	Spontaneous	Enterprising	Obstructive	
Sun—Jupiter	Content	Benevolent	Extravagant	Philosophy and luck
	Generous	Magnanimous	Ostentatious	
	Optimistic	Prophetic	Overconfident	
Sun—Saturn	Realistic	Methodical	Limited	Self-discipline
	Serious	Patient	Pessimistic	
	Stoical	Persistent	Procrastinating	

Sun—Uranus	Dynamic Individualistic Singular	Creative Independent Open-minded	Disruptive Eccentric Tense	Ability to change
Sun—Neptune	Dispersive Idealistic Intuitive	Humane Inspirational Kindly	Delusive Impractical Diffuse	Spiritual perception
Sun—Pluto	Exclusive Introspective Investigative	Cathartic Purging Self-renewing	Callous Relentless Ruthless	Regeneration
Moon—Mercury	Aware Restless Sensitive	Retentive Sentient Versatile	Forgetful Inconstant Tense	Responses
Moon—Venus	Epicurean Poised Attractive	Beautiful Graceful Refined	Hedonistic Sybaritic Uncouth	Sentiments
Moon—Mars	Passionate Forceful Intense	Enthusiastic Vivacious Zealous	Belligerent Sentimental Quarrelsome	Emotions
Moon—Jupiter	Expansive Fertile Jovial	Exuberant Happy Generous	Careless Exaggerative Wanton	Expansion of feelings

KEY TO PLANETARY ASPECTS (Continued)

Aspecting Planets	*Conjunction*	*Positive*	*Negative*	*Refers to*
Moon—Saturn	Restricted Depressive Limited	Cohesive Restrained Tenacious	Brooding Clannish Miserable	Limitation of feelings
Moon—Uranus	Electrifying Impetuous Quixotic	Fascinating Magnetic Unique	Anomalous Capricious Eccentric	Attraction to the unusual
Moon—Neptune	Fanciful Impressionable Receptive	Appreciative Perceptive Sympathetic	Diffuse Fantasizing Lazy	Reception of spiritual impulses
Moon—Pluto	Recessive Retreating Secretive	Discreet Penetrating Trenchant	Sarcastic Acrimonious Neurotic	Hidden depths
Mercury—Venus	Adaptable Cooperative Suave	Articulate Diplomatic Polished	Awkward Inarticulate Untidy	Mental refinement
Mercury—Mars	Excitable Critical Quick-witted	Agile Analytic Communicative	Fitful Irascible Petulant	Mental acuity

Mercury—Jupiter	Broad-minded Farseeing Philosophical	Discerning Humorous Sagacious	Indiscriminate Redundant Talkative	Expansion of mind
Mercury—Saturn	Determined Practical Pragmatic	Punctilious Sensible Shrewd	Exacting Inhibited Taciturn	Crystallization of ideas
Mercury—Uranus	Clever Ingenious Nonconforming	Brilliant Experimental Original	Iconoclastic Insolent Rebellious	Intuition
Mercury—Neptune	Flighty Poetic Visionary	Inventive Imaginative Theorizing	Deceptive Disorganized Vague	Imagination
Mercury—Pluto	Abrupt Eruptive Outspoken	Incisive Keen Piercing	Caustic Dictatorial Sarcastic	Secret knowledge
Venus—Mars	Amorous Erotic Passionate	Chivalrous Devoted Romantic	Seductive Fickle Maudlin	Personal pleasures
Venus—Jupiter	Exuberant Lavish Extravagant	Generous Indulgent Lucky	Excessive Profligate Wasteful	Social pleasures

KEY TO PLANETARY ASPECTS (Continued)

Aspecting Planets	*Conjunction*	*Positive*	*Negative*	*Refers to*
Venus—Saturn	Cautious	Faithful	Covetous	Control of feelings
	Judicial	Loyal	Unrelenting	
	Ritualistic	Trustworthy	Undemonstrative	
Venus—Uranus	Exotic	Bewitching	Amoral	Free expression of feelings
	Freedom-loving	Enchanting	Erratic	
	Unconventional	Exceptional	Sexually deviate	
Venus—Neptune	Artistic	Affectionate	Dissolute	Diffusion of feelings
	Glamorous	Kind	Promiscuous	
	Musical	Tender	Susceptible	
Venus—Pluto	Compulsive	Astute	Infatuated	Karmic attractions
	Fatalistic	Concerned	Money-loving	
	Profound	Sexy	Obsessed	
Mars—Jupiter	Optimistic	Cheerful	Reckless	Enthusiasm
	Eager	Vigorous	Overdoing	
	Lively	Vital	Pushing	
Mars—Saturn	Industrious	Determined	Cynical	Work
	Resolute	Enduring	Defensive	
	Tough	Indomitable	Impatient	

Mars—Uranus	Daring Headstrong Impulsive	Heroic Instigating Self-projective	Explosive Imprudent Foolhardy	Pioneering
Mars—Neptune	Dramatic Fervent Histrionic	Crusading Spirited Theatrical	Fanatic Nefarious Sadistic	Glory-seeking
Mars—Pluto	Bold Power-loving Warlike	Assertive Commanding Energetic	Bellicose Cutting Intransigent	Purifying the emotions by art
Jupiter—Saturn	Ambitious Conservative Law-abiding	Careful Disciplined Honorable	Inconsistent Manic-depressive Ponderous	Planning and organizing
Jupiter—Uranus	Egalitarian Unorthodox Unrestrained	Humanitarian Liberal Progressive	Deviant Injudicious Radical	The search for new horizons
Jupiter—Neptune	Compassionate Meditative Mystical	Comprehensive Hospitable Reverent	Elusive Escapist Overconfident	Transcendent idealism
Jupiter—Pluto	Insightful Invincible Percipient	Productive Resourceful Uplifting	Driving Inquisitorial Overambitious	Untapped resources

KEY TO PLANETARY ASPECTS (Continued)

Aspecting Planets	*Conjunction*	*Positive*	*Negative*	*Refers to*
Saturn—Uranus	Galvanic Scientific Spasmodic	Efficient Inventive Truth-seeking	Insurgent Lawless Truculent	Catalyst to transformations
Saturn—Neptune	Pensive Retiring Wistful	Atoning Propitiating Sacrificing	Frustrated Repressed Shy	Spiritual discipline
Saturn—Pluto	Cryptic Inscrutable Reclusive	Abstemious Ascetic Staunch	Austere Coercive Implacable	Regimentation
Uranus—Neptune	Metaphysical Preternatural Unearthly	Altruistic Fraternal Obliging	Eerie Grotesque Weird	The superlogic sphere
Uranus—Pluto	Catalytic Earthshaking Revolutionary	Awakening Reforming Renewing	Anarchistic Fissionable Shattering	Catalytic transitions
Neptune—Pluto	Annihilating Eradicating Pulverizing	Redemptive Regenerative Transcendent	Crumbling Decaying Disintegrating	Forces of regeneration

Index

Index

Index

Index

Index